Horses and children, I often think, have a lot of the good sense there is in the world. -- Josephine Demott Robinson

i

AMAZING GRAYS, AMAZING GRACE

Lessons in Leadership, Relationship,
and the Power of Faith
Inspired by the Love of God and Horses

LYNN BABER

Again, the early-morning sun was generous with its warmth. All the sounds dear to a horseman were around me - the snort of the horses as they cleared their throats, the gentle swish of their tails, the tinkle of irons as we flung the saddles over their backs - little sounds of no importance, but they stay in the unconscious library of memory.

-- Wynford Vaughan-Thomas

Lynn and Bo

AUTHOR'S NOTE

Many of my greatest lessons and blessings are the result of horse training - me training horses and horses training me. The simplicity of gospel concepts make them wonderful illustrations for establishing right relationship and worthy leadership with horses. Horses are far more honest and consistent study partners than other folks.

Life is a series of changing seasons. For much of my career I particularly enjoyed training stallions. You'll read a bit about that in later chapters as well as share blessings and tragedies, victories in the show pen and defeats in the loss of dear horses. I no longer train stallions, but they were instrumental to my education.

Effective communication with horses is simple, direct, consistent, and unambiguous. If there's anything special about me, it is profound simplicity.

It wasn't always that way. Some of the more interesting lessons I learned about simplicity came from stallions. The only way to get a 1500-pound mass of hairy testosterone to offer obedience and loyalty is to earn it. You can't fool God and you can't fool a horse. They can spot fake a thousand yards away.

I was blessed with wonderful clients, students, and horses. Just as I hope each of them knows how grateful I am for the trust they placed in me, let me thank you as well, for taking the time to read *Amazing Grays, Amazing Grace*. Should you be disappointed in any way, the fault is mine and not with the Author of the message.

God bless your journey.

Table of Contents

Author's Note..vii

Introduction...1

It Takes a Horse to Train a Horse 5

This Is the Promise...15

Wild Horses and the Narrow Gate....................19

Wisdom and Instruction.....................................25

In the Beginning...31

Proper Discipline 37

Unable or Unwilling?...45

Bo and Swizzle 49

Building Foundation...57

Faith in the Unseen 67

Disputable Things..73

Keep It Simple 77

Follow the Leader...83

Changed by Relationship 93

It's the Relationship, Not the Horse................111

Love and Loving Leadership 123

You Can't Fool God 127

Faith and Effort 135

Communication and Making Mistakes............147

Leadership or Domination 157

Habit or Obedience..167

The 153 Fish Principle 173

Test of Leadership 179

Obedience and Bonding 187

Leading Groups 197

Distractions 205

Correction, Not Punishment 213

I Am the Horse 219

Pretty is as Pretty Does 223

Relationship, the greatest Blessing 227

Progressive Relationship 233

Abandonment 237

The Spotted Wonder 243

About the Author 257

INTRODUCTION

The day is unveiled as the morning sun slowly rises above black-green trees and deep purple hills, each new angle of sunlight creating an original canvas upon which God's artwork appears to those awake to behold its glory. As dawn progresses, trees take on more distinct shape. Buildings appear to rise out of a flat landscape as if elevated from below.

Grass becomes a luxurious carpet of vibrant green as new sunlight refracts through droplets of morning dew. The solar spotlight illuminates vague forms of grazing horses that moments earlier were but ghostly images. My eyes search for confirmation that my little herd made it safely through the night. There is the tall black mare, powerful dun, and my two grays. All is well.

This is a day that the Lord has made; let us rejoice and be glad in it. God is faithful, bringing new life and opportunity to His family with the sunrise. I rested well last night, wrapped in the assurance that He was awake and watching over us. With dawn the responsibility for my horses passes from God to me until tonight, when the watch returns to heaven.

Have you noticed how birds sing with special joy in springtime? Their music accompanies my study as I look through my east window to the horses grazing beyond, grateful for another opportunity to walk with the Lord. My greatest blessing is being a child of God, knowing that He loves me beyond my capacity to comprehend. How can we possibly grasp unknowable depths of relationship with God and our Savior, Jesus Christ? What could possibly bridge the distance between heaven and earth to allow mere mortals a glimpse of eternity?

Grace.

The Holy Spirit gives each child of God a unique context allowing us to build a personal relationship with Him. For me, that context is horses. Twenty years training horses was my preparatory school, providing the key I needed to grasp what were only vague elements of relationship with God. The key was provided by my amazing grays, Bo and Swizzle. I chose them and they chose me. Daily lessons with the Holy Spirit allows me to direct and deepen the bond I share with my grays, just as they bless me with greater understanding of the absolute truth and promise of God's Word.

The secret of life is relationship with God. The important question is not how, why, where, or when; the important question is "Who?" This book is a collection of concepts and stories; an opportunity to discover how horses lead us closer to God. Woven into the fabric of the message are love, correction, wonderment, obedience, accountability, success, failure, birth, and death. But the heartbeat giving each life is relationship with the Lord.

Praise be to the God and Father of our Lord Jesus Christ, who has blessed us in the heavenly realms with every spiritual blessing in Christ. For He chose us in Him before the creation of the world to be holy and blameless in his sight. In love He predestined us to be adopted as His sons through Jesus Christ, in accordance with his pleasure and will—to the praise of His glorious grace, which He has freely given us in the One He loves.

And you were also included in Christ when you heard the word of truth, the gospel of your salvation. Having believed, you were marked in Him with a seal, the promised Holy Spirit, who is a deposit guaranteeing our inheritance until the redemption of those who are God's possession—to the praise of His glory. ~ Ephesians 1:3–6, 13–14

Amazing grace, how sweet the sound of my grays snuffling contentedly in their stalls, secure in the knowledge that I watch over them as He watches over me.

IT TAKES A HORSE TO TRAIN A HORSE

Watch out for false prophets... By their fruit you will know them. ~ Matthew 7:15-16

The greatest obstruction to the working of God comes from those who give themselves to interpreting the words of God rather than doing them. ~ Oswald Chambers

How many avid horse people search out books and articles about horse training? A bunch. I warn folks to watch out for two kinds of people; those who say they know all there is to know about horses and those who say they completely understand the book of Revelation. If you meet someone like that *run*! Neither is true or even possible. Anyone who believes he knows all there is to know about horses or Revelation is woefully misguided or a false teacher. Don't listen to or read another word from his lips or pen.

Facebook, MySpace, Twitter, and similar social media created the perception in many that the world anxiously awaits their next blogpost. Our collective sense of self-importance soared off the chart years ago. Indeed, when I heard that then fifteen-year-old Miley Cyrus was going to write her autobiography, I thought, *She's barely through puberty. What great wisdom could she possibly have to share?*

This potential for instant celebrity exacerbates our natural human desire to pontificate and expound upon important or popular subjects. It testifies to our innate laziness and egotism. We believe our personal insights about Scripture or horse training are brilliant. Social media lets us share thoughts and opinions without the work of crafting sentences and paragraphs, using applicable illustrations, or crediting sources.

The topics of horses and religion always attract large listening or reading audiences because no human can corner the market on them. You can read about wonderful relationships others have with the Lord or with their horse. We see evidence of such amazing relationships on television, in movies, in print, and on the Net. Evidence of these marvelous and rare relationships seem to border on the miraculous. Stories abound of miracle dogs and miracle horses. Enter either of these phrases in your favorite search engine, and the number of hits will astonish you. I did that today and came up with 48,300,000 hits for *miracle dog* and 28,100,000 for *miracle horse*. I found 789 results for *miracle horse* on Amazon.com alone.

Miracle Relationships

Are there truly miracle animals? Personally, I don't think so. Most miracle animal stories are more accurately described as miracle relationships. Such relationships are both passionate and personal. A dog so identified with the owner that it warns of an impending seizure proves the power and depth of relationship, not evidence that the dog is miraculous. The ability to predict seizures doesn't transfer readily from one person to another. The dog might be trained to react similarly for another human, but not without establishing supporting relationship with the new person first.

Do some of these stories share real miracles? Perhaps. But even if you find a case where a dog or horse performed an astonishing act in the absence of relationship with the human involved (there's nearly always a human involved), the act is an act of God, not a miracle animal. There was a recent story about a yellow Labrador retriever whose canine companion was hit by a car. The lab took hold of his friend and pulled him off the road amidst heavy traffic. Is he a miracle dog? No. The story is evidence of a special relationship between the two dogs.

Consider police K-9 units. The relationship between handler and dog is critical to the effectiveness of the dog/officer partnership. There are many moving stories of heroism and mercy that K-9 units bring to emergency situations. Police dogs live at the home of their human partners as an integral and beloved member of the family. If relationship weren't the key to success officers would simply pick up a dog at the station kennel prior to each shift.

Relationship Is Required

The amazing relationships a seeing-eye dog has with its blind owner, the police dog has with the officer, or the bond a service miniature horse has with her owner are not built by reading books or watching videos. In every case the human must be properly paired with an animal and a relationship established. The depth of relationship defines the ultimate level of service an animal will perform for a human. Sometimes no training is needed apart from a loving bond.

You cannot build relationship unless you are in a relationship. You cannot learn to train a horse without first having a horse.

Little benefit is realized if you read the Bible with no relationship to the God of the Bible. There is little benefit to anyone who listens to folks commenting on biblical or horse training issues who offers nothing but an intellectual position.

It is impossible to expound on Scripture in any meaningful way without a relationship with God. Those who share insights and commentary about training horses must have a relationship with a horse. This is the minimal requirement. Once this is established you may begin to evaluate the benefit of their opinion.

Have you participated in any equine competition at a relatively high level? If so, did you simply gather up the reins for your first ride on a new horse and win? Probably not. Equine competition is based on teamwork. One of the reasons we keep at it is because no one has ever mastered the possibilities of the horse-human partnership. To compete on horseback is to combine two separate physical bodies and personalities, then throw emotion on top to make it more interesting. You may have an off day when your horse feels fantastic. You may be on top of your game on a day your horse is out of sorts.

All horse-and-rider successes are built upon a framework of leader and follower. Most horse and rider teams need time to learn each other's personalities, forge effective methods of communication and correction, and develop trust and confidence in their mutual ability to succeed. Not just confidence for the rider or the horse as a trained athlete, but confidence in the ability of the team. Usually the rider becomes the leader and the horse the follower. There are exceptions where the horse is the leader or tutor and the rider the follower or student.

Some horses learn their jobs so well that no matter who sits in the saddle or how correct or incorrect the rider's input, the team is successful. These horses have great self-confidence and perform to a high degree from a habit of task rather than a habit of obedience. There is some mixture of the two, but if you doubt which habit provides the greatest influence, leap into the saddle and ask such a horse to perform outside its usual range of maneuvers. Chances are the horse will do as it always does and not what you ask. A perfect example of a horse with a solid habit of task is the rental trail horse. These horses follow the one in front of them no matter who or what is on their back. Getting one to deviate from its routine is next to impossible and the stable owner won't appreciate your attempt to untrain his horse.

Two types of horses are the most difficult to ride: those that are hardly trained and those that are highly trained. The barely trained horse has little ability to give or receive effective communication and the highly-trained horse is acutely responsive to tiny, often imperceptible, cues. Two ounces of excess pressure on a highly-tuned horse may result in a big, completely unexpected response. Two ounces of added pressure on the barely trained horse may get you no response at all.

Why Should You Listen to Me?

Beware of people who read the Bible and offer everyone a declaration of what the words mean or *should* mean. That person may have no experience in what he or she speaks about with such certainty. The Bible tells us not to teach others how to solve problems that we have not first lived and conquered in our own lives. Folks who read a lot about the nature of the horse and how to train one may express their views and opinions with absolute certainty and with an air of authority. But have they successfully proven their theories in the dust of the round pen or replicated their results with other horses if they were successful with one?

So, you rightly inquire, "Are you, Lynn Baber, different from such people? Why should we read your words or consider them potentially valuable?" Before I answer your question let me first make this statement: I do not know all there is to know about horses nor will I attempt to exhaustively explain the book of Revelation.

Now that I have cleared that hurdle, allow me to make my case for your review and consideration. I applaud and encourage your reluctance to consider my views without first asking about my credentials.

Over the years, I was privileged to receive instruction from dozens of horsemen and horsewomen and hundreds of horses. I learned valuable lessons from both gifted and incompetent riders. I learned from outstanding horses as well as the few rogues I trained. Psychological basics generalize to most people but we must note the mentally and emotionally unstable individuals for whom normal rules and expectations just don't apply. The same is true of horses.

Skills and abilities I learned over twenty years apply to most horses. But some horses are mentally or emotionally unbalanced. It doesn't matter if they were made that way by nature or circumstance; only seasoned professionals should work with them. Some can be rehabilitated and become useful or trustworthy horses. Many will not. I've worked with seriously unbalanced horses. Some became manageable, but only with strictly enforced routines and constant maintenance. Others learned but did not retain instruction, remaining unpredictable and potentially dangerous if their routine varied even slightly.

One of the qualities or skills good trainers cultivate is the ability to separate sane, balanced horses from those who aren't. Observable behaviors of the normal and the abnormal horse look alike to the average horse trainer or owner. The good trainer uses previous successes and failures to discern which is normal and which is not by comparing the behavior to the specific circumstances. What caused the horse's reaction? Any single stimulus or pressure will yield a normal range of responses in most horses. When a horse responds way outside that range, the good trainer will note the aberrant reaction and test to determine what situation he or she faces. Both normal and abnormal horses run, buck, and kick.

Comparing circumstances with behavior helps establish whether the response is within normal limits or not.

Not only have I proven my ability to build right relationships with horses, but I have done so with a variety of horses with great diversity of temperament, ability, and intelligence. If required, I am prepared to back up my words with action. As a horse leader, I can prove in the physical arena what I offer in the intellectual arena.

Trust but Verify

What about my illustrations and comparisons relative to relationship with God? I do not ask you to, nor would I want you to, accept my views as truth on their own merit. Read what I offer, considering all else you know intuitively or rationally. Do the concepts I present ring true to you? Do they add to or help explain facts or experiences you already have? As a horse trainer, I hope to provide you with new information or concepts. As a Christian, I hope to use life with horses to illuminate your study of Scripture as revealed by the Holy Spirit. In the same way, Oswald Chambers speaks to me and makes my relationship with Jesus Christ easier to understand on a human level, it would be a great privilege to be of similar service in a small way to you.

Relationship with our horses is a lifelong pursuit. We will never master all that potentially could be. Our work will only be finished if lose interest and quit. It's easier for me to process questions about my relationship with God when I restate the issue into trainer-horse terms. Everything becomes simple and I gain greater perspective.

When you hear or read a statement about being rightly related to God you must return to His Word to verify its accuracy. Do the same with what I write. Discover truth by going to your Bible and to the Lord in prayer.

Authenticity

Many horse trainers teach students one way to train but are observed using different and sometimes opposite methods with their own horses. If you encounter this situation find ask is a reasonable explanation for the disparity. If not, find a different trainer to emulate. Too often similar situations exist in other areas of your life—with preachers, teachers, politicians, and experts of many stripes. Is your preacher living as he preaches? If not, find another. Does the politician live by the words he or she so eloquently speaks in public? Probably not. Vote him or her out of office and find another more deserving and trustworthy. Does your physician constantly harass you about your weight and smoking? Is he a physically fit, trim, non-smoker? If your experts aren't great examples of what they preach to others, find other experts. The walk and talk must match.

Search me, O God, and know my heart; Try me, and know my anxieties; And see if there is any wicked way in me, And lead me in the way everlasting. ~ Psalm 139:23–24

My desire is to be searched by God and found absolutely authentic, living in accordance with every word I write. My personal habit is to speak as if every word will be printed on the front page of a newspaper. If I don't want it printed I try not to speak it. If there is any place where my words and behavior differ, I want to know so I can clarify my words or correct my behavior. I want to be the leader my horses believe I am. More importantly, I want to be the child God has called me to be.

The only way to learn how to fish is to fish. The only way to build great relationships is to devote regular time and significant energy to them -- and be in their company! You cannot be in a right relationship with God if you only hear His Word from the pulpit on Sunday morning. You will never build an amazing relationship with a horse if you stay indoors reading how-to books or watching training videos while your horse is out in the pasture alone.

Theodore Roosevelt said,

It is not the critic who counts; nor the man who points out how the doer of deeds could have done them better. The credit belongs to the man who is actually in the arena…who strives valiantly; who errs and comes short again and again…who at the best, knows in the end the triumph of high achievement, and who, at the worst, if he fails, at least fails while daring greatly so that his place will never be with those timid souls who know neither victory or defeat.

God asks us to be authentic and consistent. Use the same standard to select your teachers. You must have a horse to train a horse. Look for teachers who have been in the arena, who have tried time and time again, who persevered through failure and defeat until they reached a place of success and are willing to share their journey with you.

If you never come in after a day's work with manure on your boots, dirt in your nose, or sweat on your hatband, you are not a horse trainer. If you have never been stricken to the depth of your soul with the guilt of knowing that God sent His only Son to die for you, the Holy Spirit has never taken you to the woodshed. A shower will clean you up after a day in the round pen, but only the blood of Christ can clean you up from the inside out.

THIS IS THE PROMISE

If what you heard from the beginning abides in you, you also will abide in the Son and in the Father. This is the promise He has promised us—eternal life. ~ 1 John 2:24-25

Endurance is not just the ability to bear a hard thing, but to turn it into glory. ~ William Barclay (1907–1978)

Discovering the desire for freedom in Christ may be instantaneous or build over weeks or years. All who are called from the beginning will find this desire for freedom but the *how* of discovery is as unique to as our individual relationship with the Father.

...

Wild horse quietly graze in a valley washed with soft sunlight veiled by gauzy clouds spun from humidity. The only movement comes from a wild horse languidly comparing one blade of grass with another and the occasional swish of his tail in response to a solitary fly. Herd mates graze contentedly nearby. A small group of mares and foals nap in the shade of gnarled trees commonly found where homesteads were made then overgrown in decades past. The land has returned to the rabbits, quail, coyotes, and wild horses.

Suddenly, the wild horse stopped nibbling and stands motionless like a paused video image.

My senses pick up something and I stop grazing. The faintest breeze moves gently down the valley, each puff dancing on the long hairs of my muzzle. I recognize *something* and lift my head. *What is it?* Closing my eyes I lift my head higher, flaring my nostrils to gather in what the cool breeze brings.

There is something here, wait... the breeze carries something new. I take one tentative step forward then hesitate; my nostrils drinking in another draught of clear air and another—I've never breathed air like this. Without realizing it my feet had moved me forward again. I stopped. *Where is the breeze coming from?* What is the source of this scent I recognize but can't identify? I slowly move my head from side to side to locate the origin of the inviting scent.

I make one last sweep, tasting the air as I pass from left to right. *Yes, the scent is coming from beyond the hill where the sun begins its daily journey.* My hooves hesitantly move forward, one step and then another. As the scent becomes the slightest bit stronger my stride lengthens, gaining confidence that I'm going the right direction.

Moments later Soon I commit to a purposeful walk, following this strange yet familiar essence; the scent of freedom. I will follow it until I reach my destination, giving no thought to how long the journey will take or what obstacles may appear. I only know that this is the promise of freedom and I must find the way. Focused only on the path ahead I didn't see the horses napping under the tree. I will remain true to the scent of freedom and not lose my way.

. . .

16

Look, another grazing horse stopped nipping fresh green blades. She lifts her head to test the air, trying to identify what the breeze is bringing. The first wild horse remains fixated on his goal, not noticing when a young stallion in the middle of the group woke, opened his eyes and flared his nostrils to breathe the scent of the gentle breeze.

…

I don't know it yet, but I will have company on my journey to the narrow gate standing open in invitation…

…and grace will lead me home.

WILD HORSES AND THE NARROW GATE

Enter by the narrow gate: for wide is the gate and broad is the way that leads to destruction, and there are many who go in by it. Because narrow is the gate and difficult is the way which leads to life and there are few who find it. ~ Matthew 7:13–14

Your own conduct and actions have brought this upon you. This is your punishment. ~ Jeremiah 4:18, 22

The prophecies of Jeremiah are a powerful and timely reminder that human beings are not pathetic babes in the woods, but mutinous people. We live in times of devastation, war and calamities, but those who know God have this consolation, that in and above all these calamities God is working out His purposes absolutely undistressed, and although clouds and darkness are around, they know that the clouds are but the dust of His feet. ~ Oswald Chambers

It's a bad time in the world to be a wild horse. Man has severely limited the areas in which they may freely roam. With man in charge—and that *man* is the United States Government—wild horses are dying of starvation and thirst. Wild horses had it great under God's plan. As eventually happens when man's rational law takes over, a bell begins to ring ever so faintly. Over time the sound becomes

19

progressively louder until even the deafest ear can hear its death knell.

Man oversees nearly everything today: which babies are born and which are not; who will die at the end of his natural life and who will not; how parents may raise and educate their children; and how the money you earn will be spent, even if it is spent in a way morally abhorrent to you. We are like wild horses, living under the mutinous thumb of man's poor judgment. Thankfully, we who know Jesus Christ as Lord will ultimately find the gate opening to the world God intended where we may escape the bondage of man's rule to live forever, freely roaming heaven's lush green pastures.

The Scent of Freedom

Jesus tells us that the gate to freedom is narrow and few find it. Inspired by the breeze, wild horses instinctively toward that open gate. Along the way the narrow rocky trail will deliver hunger, thirst, thorn scratches and bruised hooves, yet those that recognize the scent of freedom will persevere until such freedom is theirs.

Small oases of pasture and water offer temptation in strategic places. Wild horses lingering in the ease of such moments eventually find them overcrowded and must fight one another for the remaining bits of grass and puddles of brackish water.

The path leading to the narrow gate which opens to freedom and life eternal had been blocked, seemingly forever, by an earlier stampede that caused an avalanche of massive boulders. For centuries, wild horses searched for another way out but there is none. What cleared the pathway to the gate? Jesus Christ personally removed every stone and pebble. Prior to His resurrection and ascension, the narrow gate was closed and locked, permitting no access to the freedom beyond.

Jesus Christ opened the gate, entered heaven, and the gate remains open today. The instinct to search for the path is given to some by the Spirit of God. Wild horses that do not follow the path live out their lives seeking food, water, rest, and the opportunity to procreate.

The Holy Spirit gives the scent of freedom to the horses chosen by God. As His wild horses near the gate the scent strengthens with every hoofbeat. Have you ever seen wild horses intent on getting somewhere? When they're in forward mode they don't look to the left or to the right and they don't look behind. As the lure of freedom strengthens the more fixated they become on the goal, not caring that the path has become stonier and thorn bushes closer to their heaving flanks. They press on until they are through the gate—to freedom.

Can one wild horse get another through the gate? No. A mare will offer her life for her foal unless panicked or resigned to its ultimate loss. A mare knows when her foal is too weak to keep up with the herd. She will stay with her baby if possible but abandon it when her life hangs in the balance. She goes forward with the herd to birth another foal the next spring.

Under quiet, unhurried conditions, one horse may attempt to coax his herd mate through a narrow path, rocky ravine, or roaring river. One horse will show the straggler the way and invite him to "follow the leader." The invitation is only extended so many times. If the leader is following the scent of freedom, eventually he'll abandon the unwilling horse. If the lead horse has no compelling scent of freedom, he may choose to return to his companion and they will live or die together.

Herd behavior begins to change as wild horses find circumstances more difficult. When food and water are scarce dominant horses begin to kick away those further down the pecking order. God planned for the strong to survive so when times of plenty return the strong will have mated and the herd continue.

Selecting a Mate

Humans used to choose mates in a manner somewhat like horses. Mares select the stallion they believe has the best genetics to produce vigorous foals. Women used to select husbands capable of providing food, shelter, education, and guidance to rear strong children able to help support and expand the family.

Unlike men, horses don't have the concept of self. Horses don't have the capacity to consider God's plan and reject it. Men have this option and wildly exercise it to their detriment as both the family of man and as children of God. The entire concept of reproductive freedom is that any woman (or man) has the right to make any choice they please in producing offspring with the support and endorsement of society and the government. Horses are so much smarter than we in this respect. Nearly every other mammalian society exhibits greater wisdom than man when it comes to procreation.

Man breeds weakness into his society with trend increasing at an alarming rate. God provided a plan for procreation that worked until man decided he had a better idea. As a society, we evaluated God's plan for procreation and reject it in favor of self-gratification. William Penn wrote in *Fruits of Solitude* that "Men are generally more careful of the breed of their horse and dogs than of their children."

Can a mare raise a foal on her own? No. Mares don't conceive unless they become carnally acquainted with a stallion. God's plan doesn't include test-tube stuff. Artificial insemination and embryo transfer are used in selective equine breeding because man just can't keep his hands out of the action. The result indicates we're doing a poor job indeed considering the state of horse markets since 2008.

Once carrying a foal a wild mare stays with the band of mares collected by the herd stallion. Wild mares need the stallion for protection and the herd for safety. Did you know that mares usually eat before stallions when food is in limited supply? This is God's way to preserve the health of the developing foals.

A mare on her own will not get pregnant, and if pregnant and the stallion and herd is lost, the chance of her own survival, much less that of the foal, is slim to none. But, one may ask, don't wild horses just keep mating even when times are tough? Not so much as you might think. If a mare doesn't have sufficient body condition, she will not cycle well and may not even allow a stallion near her. Even if she does mate she probably won't conceive. If she should, the embryo may be absorbed or aborted. God's plan has no error.

Something similar applies to humans. Women with insufficient body fat may fail to cycle normally or conceive. Without sufficient food for the mother to stay healthy there is obviously not enough for a baby. If a woman chooses to maintain ridiculously low levels of fat in her body due to extreme exercise commitments she may be too dedicated to her sport to be a great mother. Unlike wild mares, she has the option to change her circumstance.

Creating human embryos in laboratories weakens our "herd." An example of wild horses wisdom exceeding that of humans is Nadya Doud-Suleman Gutierez, who managed through six pregnancies to birth fourteen children via in-vitro fertilization with no father and no visible means of support. This wouldn't happen in any mammalian society operating under God's plan.

In similar circumstances, wild horses would be faced with the necessity of abandoning herd members who couldn't keep up. But then, horses aren't nearly so foolish as to get into such a fix to begin with. Most of our great societal issues and conundrums are the result of man deciding his plan was better than God's. The result is usually chaos and heartbreak.

Wild horses feed themselves because God provides the food. Wild horses work up to sixteen hours every day finding the right mixture of food to stay healthy. Wild horses exercise, play, and older horses companionably gather to watch young ones frolic about. Wild horses protect one another. They have a nearly perfect system of justice. Wild horses are obedient to God.

God gives some of the wild horses the scent of freedom. The gate to freedom is narrow. Few will enter. Most will get caught up along the way satisfying temporary urges to graze, drink, play, or be otherwise distracted in a dozen different ways. God cleared and marked the path to freedom for those He had chosen. Disobedience caused the avalanche that blocked the path. God sent His Son to clear the path of otherwise immovable boulders and open the locked gate. The gate remains open so wild horses may pass through to the freedom beyond.

Are you content to linger in the ease of the moment or will you persevere until you reach the gate Jesus left open for you? Do you recognize the scent of freedom?

WISDOM AND INSTRUCTION

The fear of the Lord is the beginning of knowledge, but fools despise wisdom and instruction. ~ Proverbs 1:7

The wise man will seek to acquire the best possible knowledge about events, but always without becoming dependent on this knowledge. To recognize the significant in the factual is wisdom. ~ Dietrich Bonhoeffer

Proverbs 1:7 speaks to the need for foundation and learning. *Amazing Grays, Amazing Grace* is filled with references to building foundation and the process of learning. Indeed, each day that passes without adding knowledge is a day wasted. The proverbial reference to the fear of the Lord is a clue that unless we walk with wisdom, the way we live our lives may have ominous ramifications for its outcome. When are we most likely to seek out wisdom and instruction? When the task or circumstance is potentially most dangerous.

Would a prudent man seek instruction before driving an Indy car at two hundred miles per hour? Would it be wise to fly a fighter jet by just winging it? Would you attempt to defuse a bomb without prior experience or education? Would you fight a two-thousand-pound bull with nothing more than a cloth cape for preparation? Would you attempt to rope and ride a one-thousand-pound wild mustang without instruction?

The answer to these questions is obviously no. Why? Because the probable outcomes are so patently disastrous that only fools would make the attempt. Yet some fools do.

Some idiots are thrilled to strap into an Indy car without instruction and gleefully push the gas pedal through the floor. Thankfully, no Indy car owner would let such a person anywhere near his or her car. Not only would the car be wrecked, but the car owner would likely be sued by the driver's survivors and possibly lose everything he or she owns. This being the case, foolish people can't easily get their hands on a real Indy car.

But I bet there's a video game simulating Indy car racing. Once the fool begins to perform well with the video game, he may think he can drive the real thing. Why? Any common sense of fear the fool may have was replaced with the belief that performance on the video game adequately judges his skill level. After all, the fool rationalizes, "I learned pretty good skills in the game so now I can drive a real racecar." Another door opens to tragedy.

Would the U.S. military offer a fighter jet to someone with no flying experience or pilot training? Of course not. Most people aren't knuckleheads and have enough wisdom to avoid such foolish enterprises. Yet, there's probably a video game about jet fighting that removes God-given fear from the foolish who confuse pretend with reality. Perhaps there is even a video game opportunity for want-to-be bullfighters.

While some may argue that all the video games mentioned in these illustrations could be considered instructive, most, to my mind, would be more accurately described as destructive. Let's consider an example I can speak to personally: riding wild mustangs.

Riding Wild Mustangs

What happens if you try to capture and ride a half-ton package of terrified bone, sinew, and muscle without wisdom or instruction? Bad things happen. Usually the horse suffers the most. Would I have any sympathy for the inexperienced fool who is severely injured should he try to rope and ride one? Not much. I would, however, feel desperately sad for the poor mustang.

Horses captured in the lonely places of the western United States are living textbooks of how to successfully be a wild horse. Whether a young horse or an adult, the fact that they survive in harsh conditions prove they have both the skill and temperament wild horses need to stay alive. A lion is not a housecat and a wild horse is not a domestic pony. Lions have developed relationships with humans and wild horses can make reliable mounts. However, not all lions make pets and not all mustangs are suited to be little Jenny's 4-H project.

A client brought me a four-year-old mustang mare for training. The mare was bad about handling her feet and had never been saddled. Once the mare and I developed a relationship she committed to becoming a willing student. Within a few months she went home to her family as a trustworthy mount for a rider with limited skills. And she was calm for the farrier to trim. This previously wild mare was completely suited to relationship with humans.

Another client introduced me to a different kind of wild horse when she brought him to me. A relatively young mustang gelding, this fellow was cute but didn't understand how to relate to humans. He wasn't overly aggressive, but I needed to establish a beginning. The first day I worked with him I could pet him and get him to stand quietly to be haltered. He learned that the best place in the world was standing patiently next to me.

Many times in my training career I earned an entire month's wages the first day. This was one of those times. That first day of training was long, but we got where we needed to go. Or so I thought.

The next morning, I went to his pen to halter and groom him before moving forward in the training process. His reaction to me coming through his gate wasn't one whit different than the day before. That silly mustang ran around like I was a mountain lion looking for breakfast. After a refresher course he agreed to relax and play. Within thirty minutes he was haltered, groomed, and ready to proceed.

I'd like to share a few more things with you, so will cut to the chase. I rode that mustang. We walked, jogged, and loped. We backed, side-passed, and rode out into the desert. But every morning he looked at me like I was a hungry lion. We could only make so much progress in the day's lesson because I had to work through every bit of his training every day.

There are lots of good mustangs out there. Unfortunately, this horse had proven his success at being wild and should have been left out in the mountains. I tried to get my customer to cut her losses but she really wanted to save this wild horse - until he bucked her off. I could work through all the stages on each ride but she couldn't. There was no way this horse would ever be a trustworthy partner for her. Unlike that other mustang mare, this one was destined to be a wild horse. He could be ridden, sure—but would he ever remember that fact from one day to the next?

Can one safely race an Indy car? Fly a fighter plane? Defuse a bomb? Does the bull ever lose? Can wild mustangs make good saddle horses?

Yes, to all the above. But in what circumstances might one hope for success? First, there must be sufficient respect (fear) for the consequences of failure before attempting any of the challenges suggested in these examples. This respect, or fear, leads the wise person to seek instruction. Which comes first, the chicken or the egg? Which comes first, wisdom to seek instruction or instruction creating wisdom?

Neither. What comes first is fear (respect) for the car, the plane, the bull, the horse. The question of practicing prudence before attempting a life-threatening task is not very controversial. We expect Indy car drivers to be experienced, fighter pilots to have the requisite instruction, and qualified horse trainers. Most rational folks should agree, but not all will. Mind you, there are plenty of fools out there who believe they are exceptions to the rule.

Choose Wisdom

It's easy for reasonable people to reach consensus about the mortal dangers inherent in flying fighter jets, diffusing bombs, and bull fighting. Could we agree on the concept that life itself includes mortal danger? Who would argue the point that all who live will ultimately die? There would be some I am sure, but as Ron White, a Texas comedian, tells his audience, "You can't fix stupid."

How many people actively seek knowledge and wisdom about something as simple as just living their lives? Life is an inherently dangerous pursuit. All men die. What then?

Learning to train horses, build foundations and relationships, is a lifelong pursuit. No one will ever master the horse. No driver will ever master the racecar. No fighter pilot will ever master the possibilities of waging war behind a cockpit windshield. Every horse is an individual and changing racetrack conditions or competitor behavior create new puzzles for Indy car drivers in each successive lap. Weather

29

and enemy combatants present ever-changing battlefields for the pilot-warrior.

The only opportunity to make it from life to life and not life to death, is a never-ending pursuit of relationship with God. The landscape of our lives creates new challenges each morning. Seeking after God requires the development of wisdom through knowledge of Him so we can evaluate constantly changing conditions and react with prudence.

Every prudent man acts with knowledge, but a fool lays open his folly. ~ Proverbs 13:16

How true. Consider the ever-expanding line-up of reality television shows like *Jackass* and *Survivor*. Not only do foolish people believe they are exceptions to the rules for the somewhat sane, but they are willing to make their case on national television and bet their lives in the process. There are foolish people in every organization, family, church, and community. They simply will not acknowledge their need for instruction and training. No one knows it all and no one knows what they don't know. Why do Olympic champions who just won several gold medals still have coaches?

If you're not an experienced horse trainer get instruction and develop a bit of wisdom before jumping on a wild horse. If not for yourself, for the sake of your family and the innocent horse you might injure or kill. Don't gamble on how your life will end without the necessary knowledge and foundation that leads to right relationship with God.

Are you a seeker hoping there's a place prepared for you in heaven? Will you bet your life on it? The Holy Spirit is ready to begin your lessons. Experience and knowledge are yours for the asking. Today is a good day to begin. And, unlike that wild mustang gelding, I hope you retain all you learn from one day to the next.

Let us seek wisdom and knowledge together.

30

IN THE BEGINNING

In the beginning God created the heavens and the earth. ~ Genesis 1:1

Look one step upward, and secure that step. ~ Unknown

My working day began when I entered the round pen occupied by a slick-coated two-year-old gray gelding with long black mane and shining tail. Before beginning our dance, I want to see how he reacts to me. Is he curious? Will he calmly look me over and watch what I do? Or will this gray youngster be fearful, quickly moving away from me, searching for a way out of this trap?

The first step in training, in relationship building, is observing the horse's response. Is he confident or fearful, aloof or panicked? Will he run from me or try to run me over?

For the next few minutes I move around the pen. I make frequent stops to look over a nearby pasture; check out wispy clouds passing overhead; quickly bend down to pick a weed

31

sprouting in the sand—doing anything except acknowledge the existence of the horse sharing the pen with me. While the charade continues, I watch Gray out of the corner of my eye, gauging his reactions to my movements. At this stage, horses usually do one of two things; get more curious about what that odd human is doing or purposefully maintain a constant distance, moving away if I invade their space. Gray started by giving me lots of space then gradually stopped moving and began to quietly watch me. Good.

This handsome gray gelding has never worn a halter. Walking directly up to him to pat his beautiful neck isn't an option yet. You can't build relationship without a method of communication. The only way to establish dialogue with Gray is through the application and removal of pressure. I must establish this cornerstone of foundation before moving forward. Body language is the language of horses. Gray doesn't know my language, so I will use his.

First, I'll ask a very simple question by applying pressure until Gray gives the correct answer. Horses learn when pressure is removed, not when it is applied. Timing is everything. The first thing I want him to learn is that pressure disappears when he looks my way. The right answer is to turn his head and look at me with his full face. Trainers must know precisely what response they want in order to precisely reward it. I specifically want Gray to turn and look at me so I can see both of his eyes at the same time. The instant He gives the right answer all pressure must cease.

Gray stands thirty feet away, half looking at me. I begin to walk toward him - he turns his eyes away. At fifteen feet, he takes a step away. I stop. He looks my way but I only see one eye. Slowly I walk toward him again. Gray turns, taking another few steps. I stop. He turns his head just enough that I see both eyes. In that second, I turn and walk quietly away. After ignoring Gray for ten seconds I turn and start walking toward his side.

This time I get within ten feet before he starts to walk away. I stop. He stops, shifts slightly, then continues walking. The intention in my step increases as I walk his way. As Gray moves around the perimeter of the round pen, I follow in a smaller circle off his hip, about ten feet to the inside. Before we close the circle he stops, nervously twitching his ears, but leaves the closest one turned toward me. I stop, then back up a step or two, focusing on his head. He turns, drawn by my backward motion. Seeing both his eyes, I turn and walk away.

As I walk away, Gray aligns his body so he is in the perfect position to walk directly to me. He stays focused.

I look at the clouds again. After counting to three I turn and deliberately take three steps toward the gray gelding. He doesn't raise his head, his eyes stay on me, and his feet don't move. I stop and turn away. After a quick count to ten, I turn halfway back to Gray and begin walking to his left.

Big brown eyes follow me until he puts his nose to the ground to sniff the sand. The moment I lose his attention I add enough pressure to get it back.

When his eyes broke from me I moved closer to his body, still walking a loose arc around him. I focus my attention on his hip, almost trying to push the air into his hindquarters to move it away as I get closer. Gray notices I am not in front of him any longer and turns to look at me. By turning his head his hip reflexively moves away from me. The moment I see both eyes I turn and walk directly away from him again. Gray takes two steps in my direction, then stops, continuing to watch me.

Gray and I have had our first meaningful conversation. When he learned that he had the power to make the pressure of my positional challenge go away, and that the right answer was to turn and quietly face me, we established a beginning.

When I work with a horse for the first time the question I ask depends on the circumstances. Where, when, why, and

33

how much pressure I apply are variables that change by the second. One very simple question is, "Will you move one foot backwards?" When one hoof moves away I remove all pressure because the horse gave the right answer. Another very simple introductory question might be, "Will you move your body to the left?" The moment the horse's nose tracks to the left and feet follow all pressure is removed. Relationship begins the first time a horse gives me the right answer.

. . .

When we first yield to God, receiving the first blush of faith in Jesus Christ as Lord, we establish a beginning. For both horse and human, the orderly process of training begins. The first steps are small ones. Lessons become more complex as new skills and concepts build upon those already learned. The foundation of relationship begins to take shape—lesson by lesson, concept by concept. As is true with a worthy trainer and horse, God is never stops training His children. There is always another lesson to learn and apply.

Obedient and amazing horses are made methodically as the trainer teaches the horse more vocabulary, establishes greater trust, and both exhibits and creates confidence and commitment. Likewise, obedient and amazing Christians are not created instantly. God provides the perfect teacher, the Holy Spirit, to tutor, quiz, challenge, and help us become the people God intends. The amazing and beautiful thing is how we can benefit and enjoy this relationship every day, at every step. Success is not a destination; it is the character and way you live your life day by day by day.

Could God instantaneously create a perfect Christian? Sure. But that wasn't His intent when He gave man his nature. There is one standout example of a nearly complete transformation; when Saul became Paul. It hasn't been repeated, so we accept that relationship with God becomes stronger with each lesson mastered and as each day shared.

Can a horse's learning process be smooth and pleasant? Absolutely. I tell folks that properly training horses is boring to watch. The process only gets exciting (and potentially dangerous) if the trainer hasn't prepared the horse. Every new lesson should so naturally follow the last that the horse only has to make a small change to get it right. Steps are small, with appropriate pressure applied so the horse's most natural physical response is the one we want. The best trainers know the most ways to accomplish the same result with a horse. If one trainer knows four ways to teach a horse to side-pass and another knows six ways, the latter is probably the better trainer. Horses are every bit as peculiar and individual in the ways they learn as people. What works with one horse will not succeed with another. Each trainer–horse relationship is unique.

Why do our lessons from God get so messy and, at times, downright painful? Is it because we don't properly prepare ourselves and insist on pursuing the wrong behavior? God never gives a free pass when we make the wrong response to His request. He applies incrementally more pressure until we "give." Pain is usually the result of outright refusal; pain is never the object of a lesson from God.

Psychic Shock

There are only three instances where I will punish a horse physically. If a horse bites, strikes, or kicks at me—no matter the situation—I will respond immediately and powerfully and in a way I hope the horse will remember. The idea is to take three seconds and apply psychic shock, making the horse believe he is in mortal danger. Once three seconds have passed I consider the matter closed—no grudge——and move on as if the bad behavior never happened. As far as the horse is concerned all is forgiven, but I pay closer attention to his body language so neither of us get hurt. Hopefully the horse will think twice before acting out again.

35

Whether the offender is a young foal who doesn't know better or a mature horse spoiled by someone who taught it to bite, I never let a serious infraction pass if I have control of the horse and plan any future with it. When a half-ton horse bites, strikes, or kicks, there is always a real possibility of severe injury or worse. In the few circumstances where a horse exhibited rude behavior toward me and I did not have control over it, I pretended not to notice its attempt to show me who was boss. Hey, if I don't see it, I have no obligation to correct it.

We've had one or two recipient mares (mares carrying foals for other mares) that were rude without me making it a big deal. These mares only stayed until they weaned their foals before returning to the reproductive clinic that supplied them. They weren't considered part of my herd and I was careful to separate them the other mares. Notable exceptions were Sarah and Hilda. They were treated like family. We made sure Sarah and Hilda went into selective programs, where they would be valued as individuals. These girls earned the right to a great life and we did our best to guarantee it when they moved on.

The horses we didn't claim, we didn't correct. If you find yourself being trained and corrected by God, consider yourself blessed with this proof of His love.

PROPER DISCIPLINE

We do not know what we should pray for as we ought… but He who searches the hearts knows what the mind of the Spirit is, because He makes intercession for the saints according to the will of God. ~ Romans 8:26-27

Grace and indulgence are not synonymous. ~ Unknown

What should you do when a horse kicks, bites, or strikes at you? This is a situation where Plan B must in place before Plan A is launched. As the trainer, the leader, I must understand my followers. I developed enough experience with horses to have a good idea of what one will do in any given situation, or at least I can compile a very short list of possible reactions. When working with a horse I often know the next move he'll make before he does. Sometimes you must think several steps in advance, taking the horse's probable reaction into consideration before making the next move. It's like playing chess.

Horse trainers must know their next action before the horse reacts to the previous one. I control the pressure and stressors on a horse in training who has a limited number of possible responses to any cue/stimulus. The horse may move left, right, forward, backward, sideways, up or down.

Knowing where a horse is likely to move its foot during a lesson is important when determining where I put mine. Horses weigh far too dance on my toes—again. It's happened a time or two. I'm only human, but I go learn from my mistakes.

When a Foal Misbehaves

When working with foals I pre-plan for our mutual safety, knowing what reaction I'll use if the foal grossly misbehaves. In a herd, mares other than the mother of a bad little actor will correct the offender when it transgresses. Great mares teach their own foals respect for their mamas as well as how to play nice with herd mates. When a mare corrects her foal, she may shove it with her head, nip it on the rear, squeal loudly, or apply a non-lethal kick or push. I do the same. I don't remember ever biting a foal, but I've sure done the rest.

Every year we had one or two little darlins' that were too big for their britches. All foals are born understanding the methods I use to correct bad baby behavior. If you don't fix bad baby behavior isn't fixed, I guarantee you'll get bad big horse behavior later.

When a foal's infraction was a big one, sometimes I squealed loudly and (pre-planned) pitched my hip into its ribcage or shoulder. My preferred target is a foal's hip. The hip has greater muscle mass than other body parts and is generally a safe place to smack a foal—but you have to be really good at evaluating body position and knowing in a split second how the foal is likely to respond so you don't get kicked. Safety first. Don't try this at home!

There are many ways to discipline a horse. Punishment is only used when there is a real danger of injury. Even with the wide range of philosophies surrounding the subject of disciplining children, folks agree that sure, swift, meaningful punishment should be attached to behaviors that may result in serious injury. When your toddler reaches his tender little hand toward the gas flame on your stovetop, you care very little about using a measured tone of voice. You yell and snatch his hand back!

Immediately following the rescue, you very sternly and emphatically state, "Never, never, never do that again! Do you understand?" Your actual intent is to scare the child half to death, making a big enough impression to last the rest of his life. This is psychic shock. Your response will be very similar if you see that same little blessing's sister running into the street as a speeding car approaches. Save the kid first, then scare the heck out of her so she lives to give you grandchildren.

Be Prepared

Punishing a horse uses the same logic. Dangerous offenses demand big responses. What if the horse is an adult stallion not a foal? Same principle, but the response will look different. I've been known to squeal at studs who also understand and respect the tone and demeanor of an angry mare. When dealing with adult horses, and especially stallions, the pre-planning part is of even greater importance.

My safety is in greater peril when a 1000- to 1500-pound hairy mass of testosterone decides to act out. Preparation is key. Every interaction and lesson must be thought out in advance. Before doing anything, I must be 90 percent sure I can accomplish my goal before applying pressure to a stallion so he chooses to yield to me. Even with this preparation there's still a 10 percent window for disaster left on the table.

I set the plan for handling the remaining 10 percent before starting the lesson. The number one rule I have for stallions is that they get no wiggle room on toeing the line of proper behavior. No breaks. No gimmees. Stallions must always behave or there will be a consequence. Mares and gelding are allowed a little leeway. I used to tell my stallions that yes, life was unfair, but the upside was they got the chance to procreate. Perhaps they considered it a reasonable trade off.

For insight on what planning is required to train horses, and especially stallions, read Luke 14:28-31. Jesus tells us no experienced builder builds or king wages war without the means to finish or win. Consider the end of the process and what is required to complete the process before beginning the process.

After a few years as a trainer I was drawn to stallions. I enjoyed them and had many in training, frequently having more stallions in the barn than geldings or mares. Stallions are easy to figure out. Stallions know their purpose. Stallions are usually direct, literal, and can make excellent students. Mares are subject to hormonal changes and not always consistent in their responses. For years, I found geldings less interesting than stallions, but now I put geldings at the top of my list of preferred horses to train. The three differences between now and then are: I have no breeding program, I no longer train other people's horses, and my interest is in building relationships. Having a stallion only makes sense if you intend to breed him.

It's true that within every good stallion there is a great gelding. Many veterinarians consider castration an emergency procedure; to be done before the owner changes his mind! From the horse's perspective, it's far better in most cases to be a gelding than a stallion. Stallions tend to be abused more than mares and geldings due to lack of understanding on the human side of the equation. Unless allowed to breed mares, there is no upside to being a stallion. This is a soapbox of mine, but I'll restrain myself. Suffice it to say that 99.9 percent of all male horses should be geldings.

And not all horse trainers are good stallion trainers. Every good stallion trainer is not a good mare trainer. Horses have personalities and gender-based physical limitations just like people. You can't push an eighteen-year-old, 80-pound female gymnast to the same physical or emotional level you can an eighteen-year-old, 220-pound male football player. Testosterone plays a significant role in muscle and bone density as well as psychological makeup.

Stallions Are Different

During my years showing halter horses I showed lots of stallions. When I started out it was challenging, since most judges didn't like women leading studs into the show pen. Twenty years ago, only two or three women in the country had enough shank power to show halter stallions. My use of the term *shank power* here is not in the political sense but in the sense that only these few women had demonstrated that they possessed the psychological makeup necessary to convince a mature stallion that he was beneath her in herd pecking order. These women could convince a stallion to cede a leadership position to them. At first, I thought such discrimination was unfair, but I determined to be successful showing stallions.

A few years later, after becoming a judge, I learned to share the opinion that most women shouldn't show stallions. Imagine my surprise. This realization provided me with insight into several other issues dealing with women in what were traditionally male roles. For now, however, I'll stay on track and limit the discussion to stallions. Most women can't dominate a stallion mentally. This isn't a judgment or criticism. It's simply a fact.

When women lead stallions into the show ring the stud often tries to sneak in a tiny rude behavior to see what happens. Little acts of disrespect were ignored or unnoticed by most ladies on the end of the leads. Many lady exhibitors had no idea that the stallions were giving them *the pony finger*. I expect you know what I mean. If not, e-mail me and I'll explain. These situations usually happened when the regular

41

trainer showed the stallion in the Open class and the woman showed in the Non-pro or Amateur class. The stallion knew perfectly well how to behave, but when the trainer wasn't in the arena the he decided to test the woman's authority. When his first little wisecrack went uncorrected, the stallion saw the opening for a little bigger "mistake."

The usual drill was that the woman didn't, or couldn't, correct the stallion in a meaningful way. His bad behavior escalated until the class was over or someone intervened to maintain safety. At one show a young stallion reared up and raked a front shoe right down a lady's face. Why did he do it? Because he could. Such behavior isn't necessarily the result of meanness; it's just a stud being a stud when left to his own devices. I don't know how many times I kept an eagle eye on an exhibitor having a turf battle with the stallion she was showing, trying to determine the exact moment I should grab the lead shank myself or send in the ring steward to prevent catastrophe.

In December 1996, I showed a long-yearling quarter horse stallion in halter at the Arizona Livestock Nationals. I led him into the arena to walk toward the judge, then trot away, so the judge could evaluate the colt's quality of movement and soundness. After that, class procedure is to squarely set up each horse in a single line (head to tail) for the judge to evaluate and mouth (check their bite). This young colt was one of the sweetest guys I'd ever had in the barn, though not one of the smartest. He was a good-looking, kind sort of colt. I didn't use a lip chain on him, which was routine at the time. He had never offered to misbehave—until I asked him to trot away from the judge that day.

Unexpectedly he reared up and waved at the crowd, knocking my cowboy hat into the dirt. Even though the young stallion was only playing, his hooves had come pretty near my face. In that split-second the judge quickly turned his back to me and I proceeded to run that colt's behind backwards with "great collection." The judge knew that correction needed to be fast and definitive. He turned around so he didn't witness the brief discussion we needed to have. After a short delay, I calmly walked my colt over to line up as usual. He won the class. In fact, the judge gave him Reserve Grand Champion.

There are many ways to discipline a stallion. We'll just leave it at that. Working with stallions is not something you should attempt by just reading up on the subject, so I'm not going to take the chance of giving anybody any ideas.

. . .

Here we are, back at the beginning. The first stage of building a meaningful relationship is communication. Once we establish a way to communicate we build vocabulary. Simple lessons become concepts. There is no substitute for consistent, regular interaction. Every time we are in the company of another, whether horse or human, we offer something new or reinforce a point already made. As good horse trainers or good parents, we are responsible for properly preparing lessons and conducting safe, confidence-building lesson experiences.

Is there an optimal time to begin training a horse? It's far easier on both horse and trainer to begin the process early. If the relationship bond is created early, the dance will be far less dusty and the degree of pressure and correction required less than when training starts later. This is true of both horses and children. When's the best time? Some authorities believe training horses starts at birth. I've done that, but prefer letting mama and baby enjoy their first 48 hours without a third wheel unless necessary.

Retraining adult horses or mature humans is difficult, requiring a higher skill level, greater patience, and exposes both student and teacher to greater danger. The probability of success isn't as high as early, correct training. When retraining mature stallion or people, there is greater natural resistance to overcome. You may have to remove old habits, skills, and methods of survival that these individuals relied on for years to replace them with new ones. Success is based on right relationship to the leader. The concept of obedience must be taught clearly, fairly, consistently, and safely. The only other possibility is dominance, which is another subject entirely and dealt with later in this book.

UNABLE OR UNWILLING?

Nevertheless not My will, but Yours, be done. ~ Luke 22:42

I must not forget to thank the difficult horses, who made my life miserable, but who were better teachers than the well-behaved school horses who raised no problems. ~ Col. Alois Podhaisky

When a horse, child, spouse, or employee does not do as we request, there are only two possible reasons to explain their behavior: they are either unable to respond as we ask or they are unwilling to respond as we ask. As the responsible party, we must be able to distinguish between the two conditions and respond appropriately. Action is always required. No response is nearly always the wrong response.

Enforcement, or punishment, will never fix inability—and no amount of education will ever fix unwillingness.

The art of leadership is determining which situation you are dealing with: one who is unable or one who is unwilling. As the leader, once the root cause is established, you must provide whatever is needed to make the follower able or provide whatever motivation leads to willingness.

What about the issue of communication? Did poor communication create inability? The leader must decide whether adequate communication was given. If it was, then the follower is using lack of communication as an excuse - an example of unwillingness. If you aren't sure if the problem is unable or unwilling, always give the horse or person the benefit of your doubt.

I've trained horses that gave me incorrect responses on purpose, trying to convince me that I had over-cued them. There are some smart horses out there, believe me. Usually the problem was one of boredom; the horse wasn't challenged enough in my lesson plan and looked for new entertainment. The horse also tested my leadership.

When a horse (or child) is unwilling to comply, we must apply an appropriate consequence every time. Education is not the fix many activists and politicians would have you believe. It is not true that "knowledge is virtue"; the belief that if only one knew the facts, one's behavior would fall right in line with prevailing ideals of right and wrong. Education never creates willingness. Education only addresses inability. The devil himself believes in God - he is fully aware of the facts. Yet the knowledge does not incline Satan to obedience because he is categorically unwilling.

Virtue standing alone is priggish. Knowledge standing alone has no application or value; it's an example of paralysis of analysis. God has a lesson plan for us. Have you already achieved the first stage in a meaningful relationship with Him? Have you established a method of communication? Do you make yourself available to His instruction in a consistent, regular manner? Are you learning to be obedient? When He asks something of you, are you able to comply? Are you willing to comply?

God knows all there is to know about applying pressure to get our attention. I assure you He can handle any tantrum we throw and has an appropriate consequence ready each time one is necessary. We are born knowing that God exists.

We are born with the language He uses to speak to us and His timing is always perfect.

Jesus Christ is the good shepherd, the best trainer. Whatever He calls you to do He will enable you to do. You only have to be willing.

Once communication is established, we have a beginning.

BO AND SWIZZLE

For where your treasure is, there your heart will be also. ~
Matthew 6:21

*I heard a neigh, Oh, such a brisk and melodious neigh it was. My
very heart leaped with the sound.* ~ Nathaniel Hawthorne

How could I be more fortunate? Through my office window
I see four beautiful horses contentedly grazing in a large
pasture that only sports this perfect shade of vibrant green in
Spring. On the far side is eight-year-old Asti, a tall, elegant
black quarter horse mare with long mane, a tail that trails
across the top of fresh grass, brilliant white socks and a full
blaze. Her right eye is the most beautiful shade of cornflower
blue. Asti always looks like she's dressed for a formal event
and stands nearly a hand taller than the two geldings, and two
hands taller than the filly. Not far from elegant Asti is my
husband's gelding Copper, busy at the buffet of fresh grasses.
Tender, sweet spring grass is a delicacy to horses used to the
dry, tough graze left by winter.

Technically, Copper is a dun quarter horse, his shiny copper-colored coat gleaming in the sun like a newly-minted penny. Copper is best described as buckskin, his coat set off by a thick black mane and tail, plenty of dun factor and black "points." Copper is built like a brick you-know-what with an intriguing mixture of refinement and massive muscle. Plus a little Disney cuteness that draws attention.

Six-year-old Copper will forever be the pesky little brother of the herd although he is the second eldest. Watching him work his way into the personal space of elegant Asti is fascinating entertainment. How does Copper get away with his little acts of blatant disrespect? Well, he doesn't always, as the occasional nicks and dings from hooves and teeth in his beautiful coat reflect. The ladies are not always amused by Copper's antics, yet he repeatedly returns to annoy them. Oddly enough, his behavior may be redefining herd social rule. I'll continue to watch, laugh, and learn.

Enjoying pasture center stage are Bo and Swizzle, my amazing grays. Why amazing? Because I never expected these two gray horses to be the ones I ended up with after twenty years training and breeding champions. When we retired from the horse industry in 2008 and built what we thought would be our final home and barn, ten horses moved with. If you asked me then which horses I would end up calling mine, I wouldn't have named either one of the grays.

Thankfully, God is smarter than I am. After a year spent caring for my aging in-laws I turned my attention back to the herd. I began to appreciate the wisdom and grace with which He gifted me with the grays. Not only are Bo and Swizzle beautiful horses, but they offered me a level of commitment to relationship I'd never dreamed of.

Asti

Elegant Asti is one of the best-trained horses I've turned out; willing to give any rider the benefit of the doubt, and possibly the most valuable horse on the place by objective appraisal. I've logged hundreds of hours on her back while working through issue after issue together, mastering skill after skill. Asti is safe for the first ride of a grandchild and the perfect school mount to help my husband with his equitation skills. I love Asti, but a part of her remains aloof, her greatest affections held in reserve for the visit of some little kid she's never met before. I guess I'm just too tall to deserve her full devotion.

Copper

Copper is Baber's horse. I should explain why I call my husband by our last name. When asked how he would like me to refer to him in this book, by "Baber" or "Larry," he was quick to select the former. I wasn't surprised. Baber doesn't like it when I use his given name. He never cared for it and for some reason he equates my use of it to a mother using her son's first and middle names when she's not particularly happy with him. So, Baber it is.

Copper has a couple of soundness issues that prevent him from doing all I want if he were one of *my* horses. He's funny, sweet, and not terribly complicated. Copper and Baber get along famously for the most part, and I'm pleased they found one other. Copper isn't the horse I thought my husband would spend his life with, but it seems God got it right again.

Bo

Bo is a five-year-old gray quarter horse gelding bred to work cattle. He wasn't even halter broke when I bought him in the middle of his two-year-old year. Most gray horses are born some other color, but Bo was rose gray from the beginning. His coat is slick and full of dark dapples. His mane and tail black. His breeder told me he was born with a lop ear and narcolepsy. They spent a great deal of time and money keeping the little guy going until he grew out of his issues. I'm so grateful they did!

Something about the way Bo naturally engaged his body intrigued me the first saw his photo - the fact that he was cute and gray didn't hurt. When we bought Copper as a long two-year-old, also untrained, I told him he would be auditioning to be "my horse." I told Bo the same thing.

With the sale of our ranch pending, building a new house, barns, and fences on one of our remote hayfields, and Baber's elderly parents requiring most of our time, Bo had less than thirty rides during the first seven months I owned him. H wasn't a quick study. He was stiff in the face, reluctant to lope, and only had one gear. He offered a rapid, stiff trot and was committed to not changing it. One of the most frequent comments I hear now is how smooth Bo appears to be at the trot and lope—and he is. When I had time to ride we worked on the most basic of basics. We paid little structured time with any of the horses for the year before my in-laws passed away in spring of 2008.

Once Bo and I had the opportunity to spend more consistent time together our relationship blossomed. Bo learned obedience and respect. I learned to appreciate his steady and secure personality. There was a time I thought he'd never learn his leads. I had to teach him maneuvers that were way ahead of my plans to get him to take the lead requested. Once we started to click, it was amazing how quickly Bo added skills and retained all I taught him.

God gave me the right horse in Bo. I haven't begun to plumb the depths of what is possible for us. Every new thing I ask of him he does willingly and (eventually) well. If one maneuver proves more difficult, Bo tries until we get the job done. We trust each other. We seek each other out. People remark on the relationship we share when they see us out on a ride or at a mounted shooting competition. Bo and I have plans. In the meantime, he amazes me.

Swizzle

The last of the four horses grazing outside my window is Swizzle, a three-year-old gray quarter horse filly bred to be a reining horse. She is barely tall enough to be considered a horse and not a pony; but she is broad, sturdy, and a looker. All four horses are well fed and well-muscled. There isn't a lightweight in the bunch, but Swizzle is more pony per inch than any of the rest, which says a lot considering the mass of the others. Swizzle is also cute. She has big, soft brown eyes; and though the gray hairs on her face will eventually prevent her white star and stripe from showing, the image they make is the reason I named her Swizzle. The star between her eyes twists about like a tiny tornado—a swizzle—before a blaze continues down her face.

Swizzle is the only who come from our breeding program. Asti, Copper, and Bo were purchased with an eye toward possible resale. I trained them all and, surprisingly, they're still with us. We intended to sell Swizzle like our other foals, but the collapsing horse market and the issues she had when started her under saddle changed the course of her life. It changed the course of mine as well. Our horses are bred to be champions. Curiously, I can no longer remember the specifics of their pedigrees. Each horse is a member of our family, so the names on their registration papers don't matter much anymore.

Not that long ago I hoped for a buyer for Swizzle. She was small, didn't quite move the way I expected, and kept dinging herself up in the pasture. The first time I tried to ride her the likelihood of selling her tanked. I had others horses I loved more than Swizzle and we had too many. God has a way of arranging circumstances. Now I am blessed with Swizzle and she became one of my amazing grays.

Swizzle was born a dark brown bay with a thick black mane and tail that rivals the hair on any My Pretty Pony. I always knew she was gray, but you couldn't tell from a distance until late in her two-year-old year. Now it's obvious, her slick graying coat accessorized with huge dark dapples. Swizzle's mane and tail are also turning gray, which at this stage means mostly black with flaxen and gray hairs sprinkled throughout her mane, and her tail lighter at the bottom but still black at the top. Every year Swizzle will sport a different look until she finally turns white in later life. I'm in no hurry. I plan to enjoy the journey Swizzle, Bo, and I will take in the coming years.

Swizzle is amazing to me in much the same way Bo is, so together they are my amazing grays. Swizzle was always a sweet filly, easy to train and eager to learn. She became the youngest member of the herd when we moved to our retirement home. As a yearling, Swizzle and Asti spent months together in pasture with two other mares. Asti adopted Swizzle, allowing her to try and nurse, which I found quite odd. Asti never had a foal, and Swizzle was in the middle of her yearling year. Did the stress of moving create their close relationship? Any thought I have is conjecture, so I'll never know the truth of their relationship.

Swizzle wasn't sold before it was time to start her under saddle. so She moved into the barn to learn new things. Swizzle had little foundation, except the basics of yielding to pressure on her hip, leading with a rope around her neck, and finally learning to lead with a halter. She had always been good about getting her feet trimmed, never forgetting anything between farrier visits. I expected Swizzle would be an easy, quick student and we would be riding together in no time. The eighteen months between weaning and two-year-old training for Swizzle was just a blur of other obligations for us, so she and I had added very little to our relationship. But the few times I worked with her she was sweet, delighted to be with me, and learned her lessons easily.

Have I mentioned how quickly horses can humble humans? I spent lots of time messing around with Swizzle, but because I thought she would be so easy to start, I took more than a few shortcuts preparing her. My program for starting colts is tried and true, but this time I didn't follow the program. Our new place didn't have a training facility, just a barn and pasture.

Let's just say it never occurred to me that Swizzle would be cold-backed, lock up, and exhibit true talent as a bucking horse. The *third* time I left the saddle without planning, I knew I needed another plan. My fault. The only high point of this day was that the third time I was ejected from the saddle I landed on my feet!

How did a wicked little bucking filly become one of my amazing grays? Grace. Swizzle is a gift of grace to me. Taking the time to build a right relationship is a gift of grace to her. In every way but one, Swizzle is the filly I expected her to be. She prefers my company to food, which says a lot about a horse.

Swizzle seeks my company more than Bo. She looks for me and is the first to run across the pasture if there's a chance for attention. Swizzle just wants to be near me and I smile every time I catch sight of her. She loves to work. She is sweet, and she continues to challenge me in ways that I am not tested in other areas of my walk with the Lord. We learn together. One day Swizzle and I may exceed the achievements Bo and I make. Time will tell. Our purpose is the journey we share. Each day of progressive relationship with my grays is a success in and of itself.

I cannot imagine two more perfect, and more different, partners than I have in my grays, Bo and Swizzle. There is one more reason I believe they are amazing: the Lord uses my relationship with them to help me understand my relationship with Him. Amazing grays, amazing grace. How can I separate the two?

BUILDING FOUNDATION

Therefore everyone who hears these words of mine and puts them into practice is like a wise man who built his house on the rock. The rains came down... But it did not fall because it had its foundation on the rock. ~ Matthew 7:24–25

The dictionary is the only place success comes before work. ~ Vince Lombardi

There is no limit to what Bo and Swizzle will do for me if I am faithful and lead correctly. When you take the time to build a proper foundation, the only way left is up.

What do I want from my amazing grays? Bo and Swizzle both have the proper foundation for basic riding and good ground manners. What do I want to prepare them for? Western riding? Reining? Dressage? What about groundwork? Tricks? High-level aires like Lippizan stallions?

Perhaps bowing— if I teach Bo to bow, I could get on without using a mounting block. As you'll discover later, I'm an orthopedic disaster and would fail the most basic pre-purchase exam. I should clarify that I've never been seriously injured by a horse. I can't say the same about motorcycles... I'm a huge advocate of mounting blocks, even for folks who are completely sound. They make life easier for both rider and horse.

The trick to building foundation is advance planning. There is no substitute for proper foundation. You can build a super nice garage on a six-inch-thick slab of concrete. However, if you buy the garage and decide to build a four-story office building on that same six-inch concrete slab, you'll encounter more than a few problems. Your foundation is inadequate to support your plans. The same is true when building organizations, education, and horse training. It's not difficult to teach most horses to go forward, stop, and turn left and right. Most horses never progress much past these basics.

If you want to compete in anything, these basics won't get you from step one to step two. Training a horse is like learning ballroom dancing. Loosely speaking, there is the proper way, the classical way, and a modern or freestyle way. What is considered proper today evolved from the classical way, and freestyle challenges existing boundaries and limits of creativity. Great dancers can successfully perform in any of the three ways.

Horsemanship and equine competition is very similar. There is the proper way, the classical way, and a freestyle way. Great horsemen can do all three. Without dedicating considerable time and study to dancing, you won't have a clue about how to evaluate differences among the couples on the dance floor. Can you judge the execution of steps, the line of the arms, the tilt of the head, the partnership between the dancers, the correctness, or lack thereof, in the actual performance?

Correctly judging a simple class like Western Pleasure or Halter (conformation) is quite complex. In a Western Pleasure class, each horse and rider perform three gaits going one way in the arena, then reverse and do the same three gaits the other way. The three gaits are walk, jog, and lope. How difficult could that be to score?

Western Pleasure is very technical regardless of how simple it appears. Many riders compete in Western Pleasure without knowing what judges look for to place exhibitors from first to last. Are the horse's gaits true? Is the horse exhibiting lift in its shoulders? Is the performance consistent, each stride the same as the one before and the one after? Does the horse move in an easy, collected manner? Does the horse present a pleasant picture, consistent frame, and natural head carriage - not too high or too low? Is the horse slow-legged and natural, or do the gaits appear manufactured?

Enough. Hopefully I've made the point that a huge amount of foundation goes into successful horse-rider relationships. This is equally true of our relationship with God. Without devoting a significant amount of time and study to this most important relationship, we have no idea of the criteria he uses to judge us. Is dancing simple? No. Is Western Pleasure simple? No. Is life simple? Reading the rulebook doesn't prepare you for dance and equine competition. Does reading the Bible alone prepare you to be a successful child of God? Once we accept that life is more complicated than we first thought, we must evaluate the strength of our foundations. What foundational planning have you done so far?

Remodeling Is Always Messy

Remember our elegant black mare, Asti. We bought her as a coming three-year-old, thinking she might make a good show horse for my husband. Asti is sired by a reserve world champion western pleasure stallion and out of a producing mare. Asti is sixteen hands tall, true black with white chrome, and a real looker. I found her on the Internet, relying on a videotape to evaluate her potential. I thought she might have the gaits necessary to succeed as a pleasure horse. The gal representing her said she had the temperament I was looking for. After a Missouri vet did the pre-purchase examination, Asti came to Texas.

I loved her the moment she backed out of the transport trailer. It was late in the evening and she was in an unfamiliar place. Asti got off the trailer, followed me quietly and confidently into the barn, entered her new stall, put her head in the feeder, and started eating. Asti never lifted her head to scan for danger and appeared to be user-friendly; exactly what we wanted.

I spent more time training Asti than any other horse in at the past ten years. When she arrived in Texas I discovered her foundation was full of holes and needed a lot of remedial work. She couldn't even lope around the round pen at liberty without falling onto her front end. She had to speed up to not fall down! When I tried to lunge her, she shot out at in front-heavy gallop. Asti even fell down a few times. The good news is she could fall sprawled like a spider and still come up sound every time. I had to undo all the training Asti came with, which wasn't much and mostly wrong. The biggest problem was her lack of confidence and the failure of leadership from a previous trainer. She had excellent manners, except for being cinchy (getting seriously annoyed when the saddle girth was tightened).

Eventually Asti and I built a new foundation of relationship. Time, repetition, and consistency expanded her repertoire of skills. Asti wasn't always thrilled with her lessons, but she wasn't all that resistant either. There were days when she was just a pill. By the end of her four-year-old year she was trustworthy, super broke, and hauled to a few shows. I didn't have time to finish her for serious competition.

In the meantime, my husband seemed to have find his own horse, so Asti wasn't needed there anymore. We were in the process of downsizing and had a contract to sell her. An odd set of circumstances kept her in our barn, none being her fault. Now we're thrilled it worked out that way. The horse my husband hoped was his life-long companion ended had too many soundness issues. We found him a good home but Baber was heartbroken and discouraged.

Asti is fun to ride and tries to figure out what each rider wants. She loves children. I'm about fifty years too old to really appeal to her. Our grandchildren ride her. Any novice can ride her. She's a great ride for anyone, from basic to upper-level maneuvers. As it turns out, Asti is exactly the horse my husband needs to work on his horsemanship skills.

Asti is the equivalent of a pleasant law-abiding person. While she is admirable and lovely, she doesn't seek committed relationship with her master. How many of us fail to achieve our full potential because we ignored or just gave lip service to God one too many times? He is faithful to keep and cherish us—as I do Asti—but the commitment on her end never quite equaled my offer. Asti is wonderful, but she just doesn't see me the way Bo and Swizzle do.

Not long ago, Bo came up to me as the horses came into the barn for breakfast. He usually waits till the mares are in their stalls and then places himself at my right elbow and "heels" until we get to his gate. This day, for whatever reason, Bo lipped my hand. That was surprising and disrespectful, way past anything that could be tolerated. I smacked him hard on his hip with my walking stick. Did he run away? Of course not. He immediately adjusted his attitude and became obedient again. Did I hold that little incident against him? Not at all. Love doesn't change. Bo repented, I forgave him, as if it never happened. My grays may be amazing, but they're not perfect and never will be. That's part of what makes our relationship so exciting.

Minnie

We had a cat at the ranch named Minnie. She was a pretty little calico; caramel, brown and black on a pure white coat. She showed up as an older kitten, taking up residence in the dog kennel a hundred feet from the house. Minnie kept my husband company while working on equipment or doing chores around the house and nearby areas. She was sweet, attentive, and cute. Of course, we adopted her. My husband is a cat guy. I like cats, but I'm more of a dog person. If any of you are cat people, you will understand the attraction my husband felt to this kitten.

We geld, spay, or neuter all animal except the horses in our breeding program. After joining the family Minnie went to the vet to be spayed. She returned the next afternoon, safely installed in an unused chain link dog kennel with big house and shaded front porch. To be sure she was comfortable and recovered well I kept an eye on her from my window.

It soon became apparent that Minnie was afraid to come out of the kennel unless there was someone to keep her company. The water bowl was thirty feet away in front of the shop building. One day while I watched, Minnie slowly made her way to the water dish, hugging the ground and looking about in fear, agonizing over every step. The slightest rustle of leaves sent her running back to the kennel. Poor little Minnie. We took pity on her and moved Minnie into the house. Years before, in Arizona, we had a house cat and worked out the litter box problem. "Never again," we promised each other. No house cats. And yet, little Minnie was in the house along with a litter box.

I shouldn't have been surprised. We have two big dogs adopted for the sole purpose of sleeping outside to chase off varmints. Both dogs ended up as couch potatoes, sleeping in our room. Reiner is afraid of the dark and Blue has sensitive skin. Neither of these big mutts showed any aptitude to identify a varmint, much less scare it off.

So Minnie, the pretty, attentive little kitten moved in. As time passed, she became more demanding. Waiting by her dish each morning she tapped her paw, impatient to be fed. Maybe she didn't really tap her paw, but I knew she wanted to. Minnie learned to use the pet door to come and go as she pleased. Thankfully, we could retire the litter box. Minnie shared our bed at night with four other little bedmates; three miniature dachshunds and one little scruffy terrier from the Omaha pound.

Was Minnie, the little rescued kitten, happy in her circumstances? I'm sure she was. She also became increasingly more entitled to the services provided by her handmaiden and butler (that would be me and my husband). Minnie felt entitled to food on demand, cat cookies (she could still be cute when she wanted to), and free rein, or should I say, reign, of the house. Minnie also became amazingly aloof, keeping in mind of course, that she was a cat. The butler and handmaiden were no longer allowed to touch her majesty, Queen Minnie. She didn't give us the time of day without food in our hand. If we managed to trap her in a corner, we could pick her up. She didn't fight, but she was never in the mood to sit with us anymore.

Relationships Are Not Unilateral

Our relationship with Minnie was strictly one way. She expected us to give, give, give. She offered nothing in return but a hearty appetite. Anything more was too much. Minnie threw up on the furniture. She scratched the daylights out of the few upholstered pieces of furniture we owned. We couldn't even lock her back outdoors without locking out the six dogs. Minnie had worn out her welcome, but we weren't ready to give up on her.

Minnie used to be connected to us, or so we thought. She looked to us for safety. She relied on us to meet her needs. We did. Now she was so secure we became servants rather than the saviors we had been to a scared stray kitten. Minnie believed she was entitled to all she desired. To try and repair the situation, I made a point of catching her once a day to spend time together. Please remember, I am not a cat person.

Minnie figured it out and stopped waiting at her food dish. I got more creative. I caught her every day and sat on the sofa with her on my lap. I talked with her, gently stroking her shiny fur trying to get her to enjoy being with us again. Minnie relaxed and sat quietly. But as soon as I took away my hand, the opportunity to exit presented itself and she was gone. We repeated this exercise again and again. Nothing changed.

Decision time came. We sold the ranch and prepared to move into a new house. There was no way we were going to take Queen Minnie to the new house, subjected to her demands for the next dozen years or more.

Minnie forgot who saved her. Minnie forgot the giver.

Her sense of entitlement grew until she considered the gifts we gave as nothing more than her due. We tried to save the relationship. She wouldn't cooperate. Minnie left.

How must God feel when He looks at us? Do we remember who saved us? Do we believe we are entitled to all we receive? Have we forgotten the source of all blessings? There's still time to work out our relationship with Him. If we don't, well, you know what happened to Minnie.

Thankfully, my grays are not like either Asti or Minnie. Asti is with us for the rest of her life. She may not offer 110 percent to our relationship, but she meets us more than halfway. We enjoy her, she is beautiful, and she has a job.

Bo and Swizzle are daily blessings. They learn from me as I learn from them. We will continue to build upon our firm foundation. The sky is the limit. Maybe we'll work on the bowing thing soon. It's a great adventure.

FAITH IN THE UNSEEN

Jesus said, "Come." And when Peter had come down out of the boat, he walked on water to go to Jesus. ~ Matthew 14:29

I know when the proposition comes from God because of its quiet insistence. When I have to weigh the pros and cons, and doubt and debate come in, I am bringing in an element that is not of God, and I come to the conclusion that the suggestion was not a right one. ~ Oswald Chambers

Loyalty to Jesus means stepping out where I don't see anything.

Evidence of loyalty from a horse, faith in the unseen, is exhibited when horses step backwards out of trailers when they can't see the ground. Or stepping into a water box without knowing if it has a bottom. A horse learns what we expect by applying quiet, gentle pressure until it obeys. When training skills aren't enough, or our lesson plan too undefined, our cues may be tentative or inconsistent causing insecurity in the horse.

Horses in this situation choose from one of three options. The first is for the horse to do nothing until more clear direction is received from the trainer. In the second, the horse weighs its options and guesses what the trainer is asking, and makes a good-faith attempt to comply. The last option is for the horse to decide that the leadership offered is insufficient and to makes a completely independent decision, judging the trainer as incompetent and unworthy of consideration.

Human trainers are capable of indecision or error. God is never indecisive or errant. In the horse-human relationship, the horse deserves the benefit of our doubt. Horses are seldom wrong. They are consistent to a fault, often to the great frustration of people who don't understand them. The blame for bad horse behavior or wrong responses usually belongs with the trainer. Sometimes a horse just says no—but it's usually obvious and even funny.

I'll share a perfect example with Arizona Sky, the first horse I owned. I was a business consultant, speaker, and active in the community. Two bad knees made it impossible to do vigorous exercise. My doctors advised against anything requiring me to stand or put pressure on my knees. Truthfully, I wasn't capable of much even if I wanted to tough it out. A young person with a lifelong habit of exercise and athletic pursuits, I was needed an outlet for my excess physical energy. I tried flying small aircraft, but an inner ear issue immediately grounded me.

One Saturday I told my husband I was looking for a stable. He asked me why. I told him I needed a place for my horse. Being an intelligent guy he asked, "What horse?" I told him I was getting a horse and would need a stall the next day. Suffice it to say, I became the proud owner of a young, never ridden liver chestnut filly on Sunday. By evening she was safely tucked in her new home at a nearby boarding stable.

Over the next six months I learned more horse training concepts, mastered the most basic of basics, and spent some time every day with my filly. Nebraska winters are a bit on the cold side. Many times Arizona Sky and I simply messed around in the indoor round pen trying to stay warm as temperatures dipped to 35 degrees below zero. I rode in my snowmobile suit, the ice on the metal doors of the enclosed arena at least six inches thick. We never missed a day's lesson when I was in town. I taught Arizona Sky how to learn. She taught me to respect "horse."

Once she had mastered learning to learn and I learned consistency and precision, we moved on to a variety of small tricks. In our routine, I gave Arizona Sky a cue and showed her the response I wanted. When she didn't give the correct response, I sent her out at a trot, letting her know she'd missed something. It was a long cold winter, so we spent hours in that indoor round pen, learning tricks and building relationship. On weekends we attracted small audiences to our little shows.

As I mentioned earlier, sometimes a horse just says no. One day Arizona Sky and I were in the round pen practicing dancing. Dancing means the same as heeling does with a dog – without halter or lead rope. No matter what I did or how quickly I whirled around to change directions - right, left, forward, backward - Arizona Sky was to remain at my right elbow. One of the most memorable moments of my horse training career occurred the day Arizona Sky just said, "No."

Our dance was getting fast and furious. I expected Arizona Sky to stop, back, roll right, swing left, faster and faster. She was keeping up until she stopped, deliberately nipped my right elbow with her lips, and looked directly into my eyes with a definite "I quit." She immediately went to the perimeter of the round pen to trot around in self-correction. It was hilarious. I also changed the lesson plan for the rest of the day.

The relationship between God and man is similar, but you must give God the benefit of your doubt. I guarantee He has no doubt. If you feel a quiet insistence, yield and obey.

When you're unsure, you have the same three options a horse has in similar circumstances.

You can do nothing until you receive more clear instruction. The difficult thing here is to determine why the instruction isn't clear. Second, you can try to figure out what the Lord wants of you, what His will is. His requests are seldom loud enough to be heard above the raucous noise of busy lives. If you're unsure, get quiet and give yourself a chance to hear clearly. Unlike a horse, you can actively seek out the Lord through prayer. If the answer doesn't come immediately, you're no worse off and you can wait until the answer comes.

Sadly, the last option is the one people usually pick. If God's message isn't coming in loud and clear or we assume a position of *tell me now, or else*, we decide that God doesn't exist, that He has somehow failed us, or that God isn't all that powerful after all. Some dismiss Him entirely.

Always give your horse the benefit of your doubt when his response is not what you expect. Redouble your efforts to be clear and precise in your requests. Precise results require precise requests. It is a sure bet the horse's failure to respond properly is the trainer's fault. The result we seek is right relationship. The loyalty we desire from our horses is built upon a strong foundation of respect, consistency, security, and trust. Strive to deserve your horse's faith and loyalty. This is how you get your horse to step out when it's unsure. Arizona Sky learned to learn and she learned to trust me.

And always give the Lord the benefit of your doubt. Increase the time and intention you dedicate to listening and reading his Word. I guarantee the fault in communication is always yours. There is no richer relationship than with Jesus Christ and no better role model for leaders than our Savior. Learn to be worthy of the faith your horse puts in your leadership.

70

There are unknown worlds of knowledge in brutes; and whenever you mark a horse or a dog with a peculiarly mild, calm, deep-seated eye, you may be sure he is an Aristotle or Kant, tranquilly speculating upon the mysteries in man. No philosopher so thoroughly comprehends us as dogs and horses. They see through us at a glance... But there is a touch of divinity even in brutes, and a special halo about a horse that should forever exempt him from indignities. As for those majestic, magisterial truck-horses of the docks, I would as soon think of striking a judge on the bench as to lay violent hand upon their holy hides. ~ Herman Melville, "Redburn. His First Voyage," 1849

DISPUTABLE THINGS

If it is possible, as much as depends on you, live peaceably with all men. ~ Romans 12:18

The optimist says the cup is half full. The pessimist says the cup is half empty. The child of God says, "My cup runneth over." ~ Anonymous

I operated a commercial horse training facility on the north side of Phoenix for ten years. Not only did I train there, but other trainers based their businesses at our ranch.

Two independent dressage trainers headquartered with me. I boarded their horses as well as their clients' and students' horses. I shared the ground rules up front to prevent friction between potentially competing trainers.

Here are the ground rules at my training facility:

1. No blood. (Still my #1 rule.)

2. Everyone is expected to get along like family. If problems arise, we will solve them peacefully, equitably, and respectfully.

3. All horses must be kept up to my standards of basic healthcare and handled with educated and humane treatment.

4. Loose dogs only allowed with prior permission.

5. If disputes became serious, it was understood that I would never leave because I lived there. Assurances were given that if a situation called for separation, I would actively help the trainer find a better situation elsewhere.

Everything proceeded smoothly for a time. Then the murmuring began. "Lynn, Lynn!" a dressage student breathlessly began, "the other trainer is abusing a horse! What are you going to do?"

The first time or two this happened I asked appropriate questions to determine what the student believed (or the trainer led them to believe) to be abusive treatment. Careful investigation of the allegation of abuse revealed that the two trainers simply used different training methods to teach horses similar skills. This is perfectly normal. The best horse trainers know the most ways to teach the same thing. Horses are as unique as people. A technique that works well with one horse causes nothing but resistance in another. What one horse thinks is punishment another horse thinks is fun. Reminds you of your kids, doesn't it?

It soon became apparent that the differences in trainer methods caused division among their students. I called a barn-wide meeting for the dressage trainers, their clients, and students. This was the first of what became dozens, if not hundreds, of instances where I used my horse religion speech.

The Horse Religion Speech

Let's assume you have a fascination with religion so you visit different places of worship. One week you attend a Catholic mass and the next a Jewish synagogue. You visit a

74

Buddhist temple the third week and a Baptist tent revival the fourth. Your investigations introduce you to observances by Muslims, Mormons, Wiccas, Shintos, and Methodists. By this time, you are so confused by religion your head is ready to explode.

Practitioners of each religion are certain they are correct. Yet they can't be; it isn't possible given the drastic differences in their beliefs. Yet each person convicted by the teachings of his faith bets his eternity on it.

The same confusion often exists in folks fascinated with horses. You pursue your interest in horses by reading books, articles, and blogs. You watch countless hours of videos, DVDs, and television shows. You spend a small fortune attending clinics, taking lessons, and driving hours to hear one more well-known clinician. Eventually arrive you're as confused as the person interested in religion.

Each trainer and his or her followers are certain they are correct—they may even have great success to prove it. Yet they can't all be right. It just isn't possible given the often-dramatic differences in their belief systems.

After explaining to clients and students that neither dressage trainer was guilty of abuse, I concluded my remarks this way: "My advice is to find people who believe the same things you do about horses. Stick with them, and give everybody else religious freedom."

As Paul wrote in Acts, "If it is possible, as much as depends on you, live peaceably with all men." The critical phrase is "as depends on you." There are absolute truths in Scripture that are not open for discussion. Others are subject to interpretation. Unless an undisputable matter is involved, choose peace with others over dispute. Always give others the benefit of your doubt.

It's the same in the horse world. There are absolute truths which no amount of discussion can change. The rest is open to opinion and disagreement. Be tolerant of others on these matters. You don't have to agree or participate. Like religion, stay with those with similar beliefs to yours and leave others in peace.

Many topics in Christianity and horsedom are truly situational or welcome a variety of options, each having its own merit. Should you worship Sunday morning or Wednesday night? Do you really believe this question has only one correct answer? Of course not. Circumstances may require a change in your historically preferred time of worship.

Do horses need to be clipped? Are gaited horses better than non-gaited horses? Should horses be shod? Should horses be blanketed in winter? Should Sunday school be taught before or during the worship service? Should communion be served with grape juice or wine? Should Christians dance?

These are all debatable issues. Find the people who share your belief systems about God and horses; give everyone else religious freedom.

KEEP IT SIMPLE

The entrance of Your words gives light; it gives understanding to the simple. ~ Psalm 119:130

It is opinions of our own which make us stupid; when we are simple we are never stupid, we discern all the time. ~ Oswald Chambers

Where in the world can man find nobility without pride, Friendship without envy, Or beauty without vanity? Here, where grace is served with muscle and strength by gentleness confined, he serves without servility; he has fought without enmity. There is nothing so powerful, nothing less violent. There is nothing so quick, nothing more patient. ~ Ronald Duncan, "The Horse," 1954

My horses help me see with eyes of simplicity—this is one of the gifts I receive from Bo and Swizzle. They let see through the eyes of a horse. Horses allow us to joyfully experience an uncommon unity of maturity, nobility and strength with child-like simplicity, honesty, and trust.

Horses are direct. They don't dissemble; they say what they mean. You'll never get more honest feedback of your leadership ability than from a horse. Paupers splat in the dirt as hard as princes when bucked off a horse. Horses don't care what you look like. Its only interest in your net worth is your ability to keep fresh hay and grain coming. Your family tree is of less interest to a horse than the fly crawling up the stall door. Political clout is meaningless to a horse. It's just you and the horse. They judge you solely on your actions. How refreshing! Can you say the same about most of your friends and family?

Getting the Upper Hoof

Horses teach more humans how to behave than humans teach horses. When an inexperienced or dull human tries to teach a horse and the horse doesn't learn, the human calls the horse stupid. The truth is the horse won. Clinton Anderson was the first person I heard who put the horse-human relationship into these simple terms: "He who controls the feet wins." In many cases, the feet that move are the feet of the human.

Human opinions blur truth and add complication to relationships where none need exist. Horses are simple. Horses are often more effective getting their desired result from humans than humans are from horses. Humans talk and pontificate, while horses look at them with amusement or disdain. Horses lean on you, they ignore you, they step into your space, and your feet move! They won.

The Stupidity of Pride

The more highly educated we are in worldly things the less simple we get. God may laugh at our delusions of grandeur, unless His emotion is more one of disgust.

One aspect of education is learning to discern the relative worth of information or concepts others present. Many have lost the ability to simultaneously evaluate information and opinion while absorbing it. Students are frequently unable to discern opinions disguised as facts in school.

It is human nature to be vain and prideful; it is not the nature of the horse. My favorite illustration of the stupidity of pride is the story of Naaman sound in 2 Kings, chapter 5. Naaman was a great commander and valiant soldier - and a leper. Decked out with fine costume, driving a gorgeous horse and chariot, Naaman went to the prophet Elisha for healing. Elisha sent a messenger out to tell Naaman to wash seven times in the Jordan River and be healed. Naaman was angry that Elisha didn't receive him personally or perform the instant on-demand cure he had in mind. Worse, Naaman had a very low opinion of the Jordan River.

Luckily for Naaman, one of his servants was not blinded by pride and self-regard. The servant said, "If the prophet had told you to do some great thing, would you not have done it? Why then won't you just go wash and be cleaned?" Naaman did and was healed.

What is it with humans? Sometimes we're more concerned with station and status than life itself. Horses are too simple to be so foolish.

Folks today are so limited in their outlook and so arrogantly dedicated to their own opinions they call you stupid (or worse) if you disagree with them. In social and political debate, throwing verbal bombs to silence opposition is commonplace. Orators pretend to stand on legal or moral high ground while pitching mud and filth in the face of any who disagree. The civility of agreeing to disagree is fast becoming a memory. How silly these warriors appear as they attempt to elevate humanity by fighting dirty. Horses would never do such an ignoble thing.

Some owners think that when their horse doesn't do as they ask, the horse is stupid. Years ago, Baber set out to bathe Sugar, our first broodmare. Sugar had hauled across the country to innumerable shows long before we bought her. Sugar knew more about wash racks than Baber. Sugar stopped when they were five feet from the broad concrete slab. Baber tried to pull her, coax her, and tap her behind the elbow. She didn't move. Dumb horse? Nope. Inexperienced leader. I don't know why Sugar resisted; she certainly wasn't upset. I suspect she wanted to see if she could be boss. It worked.

Baber asked, "What's wrong with her?"

I said, "She's being a pig."

I walked over and told Sugar what I thought of her behavior. She sweetly walked into the wash rack while Baber fumed behind us.

Every day, or maybe even every minute, a horse is accused of being stupid because it won't load into a trailer. The horse might be frightened, but sometimes the horse is just a better trainer than the human. The horse taught its owner to offer oats, carrots, cookies, or whatever, before condescending to get into the trailer. Many fat and happy dogs and horses are so dumb they won't eat plain old dog or horse food. Oats are cooked, bran is mashed, and ponykins is served dinner. I expect many parents who read this might wonder if their children have played them.

Horses win the battle for simplicity and frankness. Let me tell you how freedom and blessed simplicity adds to relationship. Some years ago, my husband discovered that he could be direct and honest without the sky falling. When a church lady asked him to dress up in costume for a play he said no. When asked why, he honestly replied, "Because I don't want to." This dear lady was surprised at his refusal, but I have been greatly blessed by his new straightforward approach.

On a few occasions over the past twenty-five years my husband resisted some event or project. I asked questions, attempting to determine the source his objection or why we were obviously unable to communicate. The day of liberation came when he gave me the same response he gave the lady at church: he just didn't want to. Simple honesty is freedom! I didn't have to keep coming up with question after question in a (useless) attempt to figure out why I wasn't getting anywhere.

We can get so caught up trying not to be negative that we create hard feelings and frustration by wandering aimlessly around a subject when "no" would have resolved the matter quickly.

"No" clearly indicates unwillingness. No amount of explanation creates willingness. Once you know you're on the same page, willingness must be addressed with a radically different strategy than inability. In most cases, folks, just drop it. You may notice that I seldom address spousal or equal relationships. Relationship with God is not one of equals, nor is mine with Bo and Swizzle. My message is one of simplicity. *Amazing Grays, Amazing Grace* isn't offered as insight or instruction on life with your spouse, although I hope you may find a helpful nugget of truth along the way.

Nothing Compares with God

Comparisons between trainer-horse relationship and God-man relationship is meaningful, yet inherently flawed. Analogy only goes so far. No relationship is directly comparable to one with God. He allows me to use the trainer-horse relationship to stay simple and focused - and as much as is humanly possible, see through His eyes. Relationships with Bo and Swizzle offer a perspective I wouldn't have otherwise. I can stand at the bottom of the staircase looking up at the same time I stand at the top of the staircase looking down. I know how the shoes of both leader and follower fit.

We learn from other humans daily, but man can't be as good a study partner as a horse. The opinions, prejudices, and influences all men bring to relationships confuse issues. You may trust that horses give you honest and consistent responses from which you may judge your own behavior.

When confronted with complex interpersonal or group dynamics, sometimes I'm at a loss knowing how to proceed to successfully resolve issues with an individual or achieve team goals. By assigning the same situation to a herd of horses, mental cobwebs sweep away and I can formulate workable plans. Horses are simple. The simplicity of children is required to enter through the narrow gate. In Matthew 18:3 Jesus says, "I tell you the truth, unless you change and become like little children, you will never enter the kingdom of heaven."

Embrace simplicity to rediscover child-like joy.

FOLLOW THE LEADER

We are more than conquerors through Him that loved us. ~
Romans 8:37

*Courage is not the absence of fear, but rather the judgment that
something else is more important than fear.* ~ Ambrose Redmoon
(James Neal Hollingsworth 1933–1996)

Horses have two distinctly different sides to their personality.
Unlike human brains, the two halves of a horse's brain are
not physically connected. When a horse learns something
with its right eye, the left eye has no clue what the right eye
learned, and vice versa.

The two sides of a horse's brain are the thinking side and
the reacting side. Experienced horse trainers are aware of this
peculiarity of horse anatomy, taking it into consideration
when developing training programs. The right side of a
horse's brain is the natural side, the side that reacts from
instinct. The left side of a horse's brain is the thinking side,
the side that is trainable and open to relationship. Even from
a non-scientific perspective this makes sense. We normally
work with horses on their near side, the left side. Many horses

aren't regularly handled from the off side, the right side, leaving that side of the brain in a more natural state. The most successful relationships with horses are modeled in a way that makes sense to the natural, or reacting, side of the brain.

Our goal is for the reacting side of the horse's brain to accept us as herd leader. We build on an instinctual foundation of relationship by training the thinking side of the brain. As the relational side of the brain becomes more dominant, a horse's reactive behavior diminishes. Innate herd mentality hardwires the natural side of the brain to play follow-the-leader. If the leader is calm, the herd will be calm. When the leader is insecure, herd members are insecure. Humans who resort to displays of anger and frustration when working with horses are telegraph insecurity and danger. Inconsistency and lack of clear direction equates with insecurity to the horse.

Horses, like most animals and people, are naturally attracted to calm, confident personalities. One must be worthy to be a good herd leader. In horse-human relationships, we are responsible for the horse's safety, not the other way around.

Fight or Flight

When confronted with conflict or other perceived danger, horses enter the fight-or-flight mode. Having the natural brain of prey animals, horses usually choose flight. The fight model clicks in if the horse is constrained from flight—backed into a corner or confined in a small area.

Another exception to flight as the response of choice is fighting another horse to establish dominance.

Humans also have the fight-or-flight response system built into our natures. We have both a thinking and reacting side. Paul tells us in Romans 8 that the Christian mind is different from the non-Christian mind. The Christian mind I refer to here is one in right relationship with God. Extreme circumstances may cause non-Christians to react to desperate situations by releasing adrenaline into the bloodstream. Something causing the fight-or-flight response to engage in non-Christians may not produce a significant increase in blood pressure in a New Creation in Christ.

The Christian is not *unaware* of the situation; the Christian is *undaunted* by the situation.

Circumstances may cause a "natural" horse or person to react in fear, to run or fight, seemingly for their lives. In contrast, the secure horse or Christian, may not acknowledge the same stressor as worthy of concern. It just isn't a big enough deal to register as a conscious event. In other situations, Christians rationally examine the circumstances, but don't immediately react. The reactive side of personality can trigger fear in horses and humans.

Confident horses and secure Christians seldom react in fear; they are trained by relationship to use the thinking side of their personality. We consider, we process, we lean upon our understanding and confidence in our leader. God is responsible for the really big things. Likewise, the horse trainer is responsible for big decisions. We are calm because our leader is calm. We are secure because our leader is secure. In the barn, Bo and Swizzle know they are safe. Christians drift off to sleep knowing that God is awake, keeping watch while they sleep.

On May 21, 20008 the Stephen Curtis Chapman family lost their beloved five-year-old daughter and sister, Maria. In a freak accident, Maria's older brother Will, ran her over when she ran to greet him on the driveway. Maria died from her injuries. Mr. Chapman is a highly regarded and awarded Christian singer/songwriter who has greatly blessed me with his musical service to the Lord.

Did this tragedy break the Chapman family? No. Did they suffer from it? Yes. Was the fight-or-flight response triggered? Will's first reaction to the tragedy was to run, but his family wouldn't let him go. Mr. Chapman resolved not to lose two children that day, the innocent son as well as the beloved youngest daughter. On *Good Morning America*, Mr. Chapman said they did not allow this tragedy to damage their faith in God. Faith in the Lord is "the hope that we are anchored to in the midst of what sometimes seems unbearable." Grief at their loss today, but joy anticipating eventual reunion with Maria.

(GMA web article of 8/6/08 by Janice Johnston and Emily Yacus.)

Fight sometimes happens when one family member blames another family member for a tragedy. Sometimes blaming God for a loss is a manifestation of the fight response. Many families ultimately fracture from such tragic blows. When reacting in a flight response, people seek escape by sinking into depression, denial, or physically leaving the family.

The proof of Paul's message, that we are more than conquerors through Christ, plays out daily in the Christian body by the power, comfort, and peace Christ offers us. This peace is one of the strongest evangelical tools Christians have for influencing non-believers. "How," the unbeliever marvels, "can that person, that family, survive such tragedy? And not merely survive, but praise God during it?"

Once they ask this question, non-believers generally follow with one of two conclusions, attempting to comprehend this nearly impossible-to-understand picture. They conclude the Christian response of sorrow-joy to be proof of mental illness or delusion or they feel a quiet, internal tug motivating the question, "How can I get what they have?"

If you think such responses are delusional, we can pray for you. If you are fortunate enough, blessed enough, to feel that tug, ask a Christian to share Christ with you. If possible, ask the very person who modeled their active faith of sorrow-joy. That's why the Chapman's told their story publicly. Inquiry into the saving grace of Christ wouldn't increase their sorrow; such inquiry increases their joy. We can't give someone what we've found, but we can stir in them a desire to find it for themselves.

Does this make sense? Let me apply this concept to horses. Sometimes it's easier to grasp concepts if they're a bit further removed from our own experience, allowing for a more objective perspective.

Becoming Fearless

Horses securely bonded to a trainer/leader do not exhibit the same fight-or-flight response to a particular stimulus as horses without such relationship. The horse doesn't need to be with its trainer to be free from concern about a situation that causes panic in other horses. The minds of the two horses are different.

Horses often react violently to sudden noises or movements that trigger the flight response. If they didn't, predators would have eaten them into extinction centuries ago. A sudden movement might be a mountain lion preparing to pounce on to their backs. Smart horses run first and check out the facts later. An odd noise could be a rattlesnake waiting to strike. Once they've bolted to a safe distance, horses will turn and see if they were right. Better safe than sorry. Such is the nature of prey animals.

My horses get too excited about such things because they've learned that sudden noises and formerly spooky stuff won't harm them. They believe I keep them safe from predators – and I do. Would they survive in the wild? I don't know. Horses that learn to rely on humans tend to remain so, even if returned to the wild.

Shame on humans to let such things happen. A year or so ago the *Quarter Horse News* published a story by a columnist who'd gone camping with her husband and horses. When they woke in the morning, about fifteen "wild horses" were there, waiting to get in the trailer and "go home." It was soul-wrenching when the horse-loving columnist and her husband had to drive the lonely horses away from the trailer to load their own. They sped away as the abandoned horses attempted to regroup and return.

My horses are fortunate. I will never abandon them. Christians are doubly blessed. No one is more faithful than our Lord.

As Bo and Swizzle learn to trust me, their flight or fight response gradually weakens until it rarely, if ever, surfaces. I deal with the thinking side of their personalities. The process is one of creating trust, building foundation, proving my leadership, then maintenance, maintenance, maintenance. Each lesson builds upon the last. Tests become more difficult as I apply greater and greater pressure to check on the gray's responses. I crack a whip at their side; they stand there. I shoot .45 caliber guns from their backs; they couldn't care less. I throw things at my horses - noisy things - and they look at me. Sometimes they yawn. If I'm not concerned, neither are they. They're becoming fearless.

A few weeks ago, I prepared to rinse Bo off after a sweaty ride. He stood quietly in the indoor concrete-walled wash rack waiting while I got organized. I expect my horses to stay where I put them, so Bo wasn't tied in the wash rack. The spray nozzle wasn't on the hose, so I fumbled with the quick-connect ends to attach the pressure nozzle. After laying the nozzle down on the concrete floor I turned on the water. Apparently, I didn't attach the nozzle correctly. A sudden burst of pressurized water shot the nozzle off the end of the hose like a projectile and sounded like a bomb.

This all happened beside Bo's hind feet. I fully expected him to bolt away to a safe distance before checking to see if I'd survived the blast. I am both humbled and ashamed to say admit I was surprised when his only reaction was to clamp his tail tightly to his butt and assume a readiness posture as he waited for me to give direction. He never moved a foot. I was humbled by this testament to the change in Bo's nature. I am ashamed that I was surprised. What did I do next? I pretended that nothing unusual had happened, paid more attention to how I connected the nozzle, and gave Bo his bath.

Mounted shooters have to carry balloons. If you don't think that's a testament to the trust our horses place in relationship, try it yourself on a new horse. Forget that - don't try it unless you know what you're doing. Balloons move, especially on windy days, and they will "touch" a horse when he isn't expecting it. I've seen the flight response kick in more than once when a horse met a balloon. Do you really appreciate the confidence a horse has in its rider to carry a parade flag? Horses with great leader learn to ignore helicopters hovering over their heads, firecrackers going off at their heels, and most any other scenario you can imagine.

As children of God, we are changed by the relationship we share with Him. New habits born of this relationship allow us to truly understand what Jesus means when he tells us to "Fear not." ~ Corrie Ten Boom

You may already be familiar with Corrie ten Boom, a Dutch Christian survivor of the Nazi concentration camps. Her book, *The Hiding Place*, shares her family's story of hiding Jews in their home during World War II. Their efforts saved an estimated eight hundred Jews from the Nazis but resulted in the arrest and imprisonment of Corrie; her father, Casper;

and sister, Betsie. Casper and Betsie died in the camps, but Corrie survived to tell their story.

Here are a few of Corrie's words about her experience in Ravensbruck, taken from a letter she wrote in 1974.

We may have been the Lord's only representatives in that place of hatred, yet because of our presence there, things changed. Betsie and I, in the concentration camp, prayed that God would heal Betsie who was so weak and sick.

"Yes, the Lord will heal me," Betsie said with confidence. She died the next day, and I could not understand it. They laid her thin body on the concrete floor along with all the other corpses of the women who died that day. It was hard for me to understand, to believe that God had a purpose for all that. Yet, because of Betsie's death, today I am traveling the world telling people about Jesus.

Corrie's message to her fellow prisoners is that "Jesus is Victor" and "There is no pit so deep that God's love is not deeper still." Speaking to a congregation in Africa destined for eventual martyrdom, Corrie told this story from her childhood as congregants wondered fearfully if they would be next to die. Many did.

"When I was a little girl, I went to my father and said, 'Daddy, I am afraid I will never be strong enough to be a martyr for Jesus Christ.'"

"Tell me," said Father, "when you take a train trip to Amsterdam, when do I give you the money for the ticket? Three weeks before?"

"No, Daddy, you give me the money for the ticket just before we get on the train."

"That is right," my father said, "and so it is with God's strength. Our Father in Heaven knows when you will need the strength to be a martyr for Jesus Christ. He will supply all you need—just in time."

Like Corrie Ten Boom, we are more than conquerors through Him who loves us. Tribulations are just another test. Although greater pressure may be applied, our leader always provides the possibility of release. The Christian in right relationship to God is not consumed by fear. What may cause your horse to run off a cliff won't get mine to bat an eyelash. What causes one person to slide into despair and depression may not cause the Christian to lose even an hour of sleep.

Oswald Chambers said, "The saint never knows the joy of the Lord despite tribulation, but because of it." What a gift we have received.

The Christian lives in a completely different reality from the non-Christian. We are different. We are never abandoned to fend for ourselves once Christ has claimed us. One day that trailer will load up and head for home. As were the abandoned horses, many will be left watching as we head home, tucked securely into that trailer, destination heaven.

CHANGED BY RELATIONSHIP

For whom he foreknew, He also predestined to be conformed to the image of His Son. Moreover whom He predestined, these He also called; whom He called, these He also justified; and whom He justified, these He also glorified ~ Romans 8:29-30

The individuality remains, but the mainspring, the ruling disposition, is radically altered. The same human body remains, but the old satanic right to myself is destroyed. ~ Oswald Chambers

Each day is a new life, from the birth of morning at wake-up to the death of evening and sleep. We are made to come to God for our daily bread (Luke 11:3) whether the food is spiritual, mental, physical, or literal. It is said that if we live each day as if it were our last, one day we would most certainly be correct. Jesus cautions us not to worry about tomorrow; today is the only guarantee. Horses don't worry about whether the grass will still be green tomorrow or if the water barrel will still be filled. Who is wiser?

Am I as faithful as Bo and Swizzle, indeed, all four of our horses? They enjoy the safety and company of their small herd, yet eagerly await my coming each morning. As I open their stall gates in, they briskly come - sometimes at a full gallop! They have plenty of food and water; they have society; they have freedom, yet as soon as they see me, they come running. And not just in the mornings. No matter what time of day, expected or not, if I appear bound for the barn, or anywhere they have access, the horses come. Especially Swizzle.

As our relationships deepen my grays take on more of the mannerisms, habits, and behaviors that I teach them. They give up more natural freedoms. Or so it appears to the uninitiated. Obedience is only real if there is the opportunity to *not* obey. I value their submission so greatly because *they have a choice*. Freedom is behind them in the open fields, but they choose me.

Why do Bo and Swizzle choose me over freedom? It can't be just food; they have food and water in the pasture. They choose me because they accept me as their leader, the source of safety, mental stimulation, entertainment, and affection. We have relationship.

It's easy for Bo and Swizzle to trust me to make the big decisions in life. It's comforting knowing the rules and the security of boundaries. Horses are prey animals. I make them safe. Bo and Swizzle can *be still and know that I am*.

Be Still, and Know That I Am God

Seeking Christians find some concepts of right relationship with God difficult to understand and more difficult to apply. As a one-time seeker myself, I understand the mindset and bewilderment that goes with that territory. Though now I'm found, I owe much of my enlightenment to relationship with horses and the insights those relationships provide. Psalm 46:10 is an oft-quoted verse; profound and multi-layered, offering valuable insight and security to those who examine it with the simplicity of a child - or a horse. There are two distinct ways you can read this verse, two ways in which we can be comforted and strengthen our faith and relationship with God.

The first way is to read the verse as "Be still, and know that I am. (Signed) God."

This may be interpreted as "Rest... I am awake. (Signed) your Father." This is a message of safety and security. As a small child, did you ever awake suddenly from a sound sleep and were instantly afraid? Then you heard the quiet voices of your parents in the next room and realized you were not alone; you were protected and, greatly reassured, drifted peacefully back to sleep.

Victor Hugo, author of *Les Miserables*, wrote, "Have courage for the great sorrows of life and patience for the small ones; and when you have laboriously accomplished your daily task, go to sleep in peace. God is awake."

The second way we may interpret this verse is, "Be still! Know that I am God." This version may be understood as, "Be quiet and sit down! I will do what I say. You need only wait." This message is one of authority and promise. God is who he says he is, and can do what he says he can. We are not to worry about anything but our daily tasks and maintaining right relationship with him.

Bo and Swizzle look to me for their daily needs, taking on more attributes of this new nature. Yet both retain their own personalities. I delight in the nuance of their differences. Bo and Swizzle remain truly equine, yet distinctly different from their original prey natures.

Every horse has a unique personality, just like humans. God delights in our uniqueness - watching us become all he knows we can be, maximizing the possibilities of his design.

The Error of Asking Why

Do Bo and Swizzle ever backslide? Yes, but not often. Each occurrence shows me where our relationship needs work, where vulnerability and temptation lie. To be honest, the fault is usually mine for not devoting enough time and attention to our relationship. Bo and Swizzle are always ready; I'm the one who gets sidetracked by events in other areas of my life. For that matter, you may ask if I ever backslide in my relationship with God. Yes, I do. Again, the fault is mine.

Whether due to arrogance or lack of trust in God, I still find myself in error, of thinking independently of God and His direction. As is the case with my grays, these times reveal the need to strengthen my relationship with the Lord. Once you're rightly related to God, you no longer ask, "Why?" When addressing God and you begin with why, you can bet you're in the wrong frame of mind or spirit. Immediately we ask "Why?" we are in relational error with God. My horses are not to ask why as if I answered to them. They are to obey, trust, and be confident in my ability to provide leadership.

The question "Why?" in many cases is translated, "Give me your reasons, and I'll decide if I agree." I don't lead Bo and Swizzle by committee, and you may be certain God has a similar point of view. Each of us has a place (or places) where it's difficult trusting the Lord's plan without wanting to know why He does as He does. Where do you still ask why?

Everyone in North Texas received wonderful amounts of rain this past week. Some areas got way more than they wanted and we got precious little. "Why," I asked yet again, "did the rain go north of us, or south of us, or miss us by what seems like inches to the west or east? Why is it becoming normal for rain to mysteriously evaporate only a mile or two before it gets here? Why don't we get the rain? Is it something we've done?"

Oops, perhaps that's the reason why. The lack of rain is a recurrent issue where I am guilty of not trusting God. I believe He'll send the amount of rain we need. But I haven't completely blocked that nagging feeling of discontent or disappointment when rain is so close yet passes by without blessing our pastures.

It is so easy to stray. I know there is only one who can make it rain—or make it stop. God is on His throne and I am blessed, so why can't I eliminate that little voice asking "why"? Did you catch that? I was asking "why" about "why." (Oh, what tangled webs we weave…) Are we guilty of being more thankful for the blessings God bestows upon us, or are we grateful for the relationship we share with Him? What a fine distinction there is between loyalty to what God says and loyalty to who He is. Would I ever master it?

As far as rain goes, yes. The secret was going cold turkey. I quit worrying about rain on the pastures. I have the tools and the responsibility to keep the lawn watered. I have zero ability to make it rain on the fields. After prayer, I realized I never turned that problem over to God…not really. I did. I am relieved to say that I don't worry about rain anymore. We've also had a lot more of it since I quit thinking about it. Hmmm.

The blessing of relationship isn't provided through familiarity with Scripture but through familiarity with the Author. Our task is to obey God, not understand Him. There is a place in relationship with our horses where they trust and obey and no longer ask why. There's no advancement beyond that for Bo and Swizzle. As children of God we will one day be privileged to understand the "whys" of all that we experience in this earthly journey. We may not have all the answers on this side of eternity, but we may be confident they will come.

Self-Esteem

Yesterday we trailered Swizzle and Copper to a friend's property. Swizzle needs to be hauled; to get away from her home environment and see more of the world. Many horse owners think that this is a process of desensitization.

Desensitization is exposing horses to different objects and environments so they learn not to be afraid of them. It's impossible to introduce every possible object, noise, and location to your horse. The purpose in hauling Swizzle is to test her trust in me. By placing her in a potentially stressful situation I'll learn if she'll maintain her focus on me or gets distracted or fearful by the unfamiliar. My goal is building Swizzle's confidence in me as her leader, so regardless of object, place, or situation, she'll be secure and look to me for direction. I intend to short-circuit her natural fight-or-flight response.

Confidence is only gained when we are tested and succeed. One of the great lies in our culture today is that self-esteem comes from a lack of failure. Wrong. Self-esteem is built by overcoming failure. Confidence and self-esteem come from the same foundation.

Our confidence in God does not grow because our circumstances are smooth and challenges kept to a minimum; our confidence grows when we come to the end of our limits and fail, when God moves in to elevate us, to turn failure into success, to turn principle into faith.

Working Out What He Works In

Everyone who spends time around preachers or reads Christian devotional material is familiar with the concept "working out what He works in." Be brutally honest with yourself. Do you really understand what it means? For many, it's too abstract to apply. We get close to putting the pieces together but miss nailing it completely. We believe our salvation was purchased by the finished work of Christ on the cross and we are indwelt with the Holy Spirit. But how do we work *it out*?

Relationship with God is worked out through trial, error, correction, and success. We go through trials, we make mistakes, God corrects us and obedience leads to success.

The truth is, God loves us to the end of our disobedience and past, until we eventually achieve success. In 1 Corinthians 4:8, Paul tells us "we are hard-pressed on every side, yet not crushed; we are perplexed, but not in despair." We should expect, even welcome, trials. If the lessons keep coming, we're still in His training program.

The first time I took Bo on a competitive trail ride I learned what "working out what is worked in" means. Bo began in his usual way, soft and obedient. He'd been on one other big trail ride, but it was nothing compared to the natural obstacles we encountered on this ride. The trail dropped down narrow paths so steep they were nearly vertical. I almost laid back on Bo's rump to give him a chance to balance as he gamely negotiated our descent. I was so proud of him.

Once you go down, it's a safe bet that somewhere you'll go back up. Up we went, where the path was rock and bits of shale between tall trees. Slippery stones shifted when Bo moved his hooves on the loose material, carefully picking his way in this unfamiliar environment. Doing my best to help Bo balance I leaned forward along his neck, grasping a handful of mane behind his ears. Allow green horses to climb at anything faster than a walk, I asked Bo to think his way along and up. He nearly had to buck up the trail to gain enough momentum to get over the top and on to more level ground.

Except for small bits of fussiness, Bo was good until we reached the midpoint of the ride. Bo doesn't get fussy, so I knew our relationship was strained, I didn't realize how much. The middle of the ride passed the starting point then continued in the opposite direction from where we began. That meant passing all our parked trailers when we transitioned from the rocky part of the ride toward the river. Bo must have thought it was time to go back to the trailer because he was completely undone at the next obstacle. We didn't have a wreck, the got a zero score on the obstacle. We didn't cause a scene, but neither was Bo obedient. Bo could have done the obstacle without twitching an ear, but he was pushy and non- responsive. Bo wasn't "with" me any longer.

Shortly after the botched obstacle, we rode through a large pasture with parallel logs placed about thirty feet apart. Please understand, Bo can jump, Bo does arena trail, and Bo will go over or through poles or logs on the ground no matter how oddly configured. Bo got to the first log then stopped and snorted as if he expected it to suddenly open jaws and devour him. If you've ridden horses enough, you know how far they can lean backwards when they don't want to go forward. Their feet don't move, but in profile, they look like they're slipping backwards down a steep hill, neck and nose stretched way out and down in front of them. Bo categorically refused to go over the logs.

Obedience had left the building. I dismounted, got out my lead rope and snapped it to Bo's rope halter. I tied the reins through the swell of the saddle and put Bo into a familiar exercise. I asked him to trot softly and politely in the direction I pointed, then roll back over his hocks to go the opposite way. In this exercise, I seldom let a horse make a full circle around me; the goal is obedience, not fatigue. The lead rope is only eight or ten feet long, so a horse must be soft to perform the exercise well. It took a few minutes for Bo to "see" me again and decompress. I knew he wasn't back with me 100 percent, but time was wasting and Baber and Copper were waiting.

After remounting, Bo and I walked over the logs and headed toward the next obstacle. The trail continued up and down, soft banks winding among low tree branches. Trees in our part of Texas aren't as tall as ones up north, so it was a pretty cramped path. The river would be coming up soon Our directions were to enter the river, circle around markers placed in the middle, then return to the bank and continue. I had little confidence that Bo would do the river obstacle well in his present frame of mind, but since he does love to play in water, I had some hope we would come to an understanding. I'd never ridden Bo through water and hoped for good footing and clear water.

As we came around and down the trail to where trees finally opened enough to see ahead, I saw the water's edge only twenty feet away. No time to prepare. I got my first glimpse of the wide, mucky, suck-your-boots-off-sticky bank and muddy brown Paluxy River. Standing on dry land well away from the river I asked the judge how deep the water was.

He answered, "About belly or chest high on your horse."

I figured I'd give Bo one shot at it but not press the issue if he wasn't keen on the idea. With no opportunity to work through a refusal, I had no choice but to make only a minor request. To be honest, I really didn't want my saddle and boots completely trashed. Not surprisingly, Bo refused.

While I wasn't particularly saddened that we didn't get to enjoy the water feature, I was disappointed in Bo's response. Our relationship is amazing because we're both committed. Bo's seemed to be slipping and I began considering my options. We wound through more woods before emerging into a clearing leading to the final obstacle, the Texas Vine. Vines hung from a horizontal pole suspended between two exceptionally large trees. Each vine was a rubber hose or plastic rope spaced about two inches apart. The obstacle required Bo to walk quietly through the vine curtain.

A hundred and fifty feet before the vines we encountered four short landscape timbers arranged in a box on the grass, forming the outline of a small square about thirty inches across. I figured walking Bo through the box should be a piece of cake, giving me the opportunity to remind him that he knows how to do all these things.

101

As you may have already guessed, Bo didn't walk through the box. He snorted and tried to slip around the box. I was taken aback. How did we get so far off track in such a short time? And more importantly, what was I going to do about it? There could be no further "if" in Bo's response or I would deserve to lose my role of leader. Bo was not obedient and I require obedience from him. I asked him repeatedly to walk through the box. Bo repeatedly offered to go around the box but would not go forward. Using the vocabulary of applying and releasing pressure, I told Bo that the only way he was going to move from that spot, dead in front of the box, was to walk forward through it.

A Line in the Sand

My directions were given precisely allowing no wiggle room. When Bo tried to move to the right he ran into my right leg. When he tried to escape to the left he ran into my left leg. When he tried to back up he ran into both my legs. Every door was closed to Bo but the one directly in front of him. If you sat in a lawn chair with a glass of iced tea watching our exchange, you wouldn't have noticed anything particularly interesting. Bo didn't explode and I didn't punish him. There was simply no option on earth other than Bo walking through the box. No matter how long it took, I would stay with him until he worked it out.

Bo got the message. His body softened, he let out a deep sigh, then politely and confidently walked through the box like he'd done it daily since birth. Bo was back.

The Texas Vines were directly ahead. I had a plan. I asked to walk toward the vines. When we were about ten feet away, I sat down, said whoa, and Bo obediently stopped. After a few seconds passed, I asked him to calmly walk forward again. He did. When only four feet separated his nose from the vines, I sat down again and Bo politely stopped. The test came: I quietly asked Bo to go forward, and he did. Bo pushed his soft little gray nose through the vines and walked on as if they weren't even there.

Bo taught me what it means to "work out what he works in." Bo is my family. I chose him and Swizzle to be related to me as long as they live, and they chose me. Nothing is more important than the quality of our relationship. Bo never left the relationship, but his original nature took over, causing disobedience. I would not lose him. I love Bo past his capacity to be disobedient. I am committed. Why didn't I love Minnie enough to keep her in the family? Because Minnie was not a chosen one. Minnie had every opportunity to enjoy a cushy life with a loving family. Minnie chose not to be related to me.

I offered. Minnie said, "No."

I said, "Have it your way."

Bo went through trial, made errors, received correction, and achieved success. Bo and I were rightly related again, his old nature packed away. Every time he overcomes his old nature, our relationship strengthens. God sends us trials and challenges and allows us to commit to the error of disobedience. God's love will never be exhausted before we come to the end of our disobedience, resulting in greater and richer relationship than ever.

Jesus "loved his own who were in the world, he loved them to the end" (John 13:1).

Disposable Relationships

Inexhaustible love is a characteristic unique to chosen relationship. No matter what, I will love Bo and Swizzle past any issues that arise; our relationships are not disposable. I wager that 80 percent of marriages today find both bride and groom admitting, even as they prepare to exchange vows, that they are consciously entering a disposable relationship. The marriage will last until one does something the other considers a deal breaker or until a better opportunity comes along.

Just as inexhaustible love is a characteristic of chosen relationships, so is exceptional commitment. No disobedience from Bo or Swizzle goes unanswered. Doing so is leadership failure. Leadership isn't a part-time job. Commitment must be complete.

When parents allow young children to disobey instruction without consequence, it is evidence of either disposable relationship or parents without adequate leadership skills. Parents or horse owners who fail to correct acts of disobedience are either *unable* to lead or *unwilling* to lead. If unwilling, the sad fact is that the horse or child isn't important enough to do what is required to keep the relationship on healthy terms.

Nothing can destroy chosen relationships between individuals. Both spirits have confidence in the worth and nature of the other. The relationship has withstood the tests and trials of independence, success, failure, and the unexpected. Nothing on earth will change the commitment each made to the other. How many of your relationships are chosen ones? How many are disposable? Let me repeat: in chosen relationships, both spirits have reason to be confident in the worth and nature of each other.

One might think that the parent-child relationship is a chosen one. Perhaps, but not necessarily. How many parents die estranged from their children? We've all known parents who withdrew their love from a child for one reason or another. Similarly, children may withdraw love from a parent when some issue becomes more important than the relationship.

God knew us before we were born. Our relationship with Him is the sole exception of chosen relationship created before relationship was consciously entered. Maybe we did know God before birth, already committed to relationship. All other relationships are built from the bottom up, from a first introduction or by birth.

The extent we'll go to preserve relationships we choose for life is almost, but not quite, limitless. A characteristic of disposable relationships is that the one in leadership works at guiding and correcting the follower until the work required exceeds the perceived benefit. When we allow disobedience or error to go completely uncorrected, we admit the relationship is disposable. There is a wide range of corrections, both by type and degree, employed as we build relationships with followers. Unnatural relationship also exists where the one in power is unbalanced or evil and will sacrifice the life of the follower to prevent a failure of relationship. An example of an unnatural relationship is the parent who murders his/her child to save it.

To fully understand the depth of commitment involved in chosen relationships, we have as the only pure example God and His children. As we learn in Romans, nothing can separate us from the love of God. There is no circumstance in which His chosen will be bounced from the training program or fail to find and pass through the narrow gate to freedom. God loves us past every trying circumstance, though there's no guarantee the journey will always be easy. A lot depends on how quickly we master lessons encountered along the way.

In the musical version of *Les Miserables*, Jean Val Jean reflects from his deathbed, "To love another person is to see the face of God." Jean Val Jean had a chosen relationship with his adopted daughter, Cosette. When you recognize the significance of the inexhaustible commitment you make in chosen loving relationship with another, you are blessed with a glimpse of God's face. I was blessed with one small peek when Bo and I approached the Texas Vines.

Some may ask, "What do I do when I have chosen a relationship but the other party shut me out?" First, remember that the relationships we're discussing have already been proven to be worthy. There's only one way to address one-sided relationships. Imagine there a bridge between you and the one you have committed to love no matter what. Midway across the bridge, the other individual erected a barrier you cannot breach. She may continuously pile more rubble on her side, making it difficult to cross back over the bridge.

You can't do anything to clear out her side of the bridge, but your resolve to keep your side of the bridge clear, swept, and spotless is evidence of your commitment. In the event the other individual decides to return to you, she need only get past her own junk before reaching the clean slate on your side of the bridge.

Forever Changed

There is no limit to the relationships I treasure with Bo and Swizzle. They are secure as my chosen grays. Through them I am blessed by greater understanding of how much my Father in heaven has committed to me. The greatest concept I learned while writing of this book is what chosen relationship truly means and that God will love me past anything I could ever come up with, *no matter what*.

Through relationship, my grays have radically altered the ruling disposition born into every prey animal. This change couldn't have happened without my influence as leader and teacher. Like Bo and Swizzle, human sin nature is radically altered only by the work of Jesus Christ and the Holy Spirit. As children of God, what maximizes the possibilities of our design is the leadership and teaching God provides. Once chosen, God will never lose us. Throughout the rest of our lives we work out what He has worked in.

"I have learned to learn!"

My own nature was radically altered from the thoroughly sinful natural person I used to be through the persistent faithfulness of the Holy Spirit. The level of teamwork we have been able to achieve—His leadership and my obedient followership—is at a level I could never imagine until I experienced it. Yet what level of training have I really reached? The summit? Hardly. I don't know if I'm a one or an eight on a scale of one to ten. Such evaluation isn't mine to make or know. I am simply responsible for my daily tasks and staying focused on Jesus Christ.

What does more advanced training look like? First, I prove I'm trainable. Once I've mastered elementary and secondary skill levels, my trainer becomes more confident that I have the heart and desire to achieve more. Horses who achieve the highest levels of performance aren't always those with the most natural talent. One frequently sees a horse with more drive and heart, led by a faithful trainer, win championships over horses with greater talent. Horses that learn how to learn and begin to love the process are the horses who outperform horses with extraordinary ability but no desire or little heart. My desire to be in relationship with Jesus Christ is a matter of heart, not aptitude.

He makes me able. I bring willingness.

Practice Makes Perfect

A 1996 research project by K.A. Ericsson studied the correlation between exceptional performance and deliberate practice. Who hasn't watched a musician, athlete, or equestrian performing before an audience nearly frozen with awe and delight. The execution of amazing skill appears so effortless we assume it's primarily due to special talent. We may even think such performers are freaks of nature when we consider the level of excellence they have achieved.

The research proved that the main influence on achievement level of exceptional performers is the number of hours spent in solitary practice of their specific skill. The most exceptional musicians spent approximately ten thousand hours in practice, the lesser-accomplished professionals about five thousand hours, and the serious amateurs about two thousand hours. The study concluded that the accumulated amount of deliberate practice is closely related to the attained level of performance.

I believe the study conclusions apply to relationships as well as performers. Saints and great horses aren't made overnight. Horses finely tuned to the breath and spirit of their riders aren't products of accident or luck. Deliberate practice with your horse yields higher levels of performance. Likewise, time spent in the tutelage of the Spirit creates greater obedience and relationship to God.

As I learned to learn, my Trainer helped me achieve smaller goals of task and obedience. I love the process. With each new concept my Trainer presents, it's easier for me to understand the next. The obedience I bring, led by the skill of my Trainer, creates a synergy of relationship that lets me master new and more complicated obstacles and maneuvers.

Do I know the final goal my Trainer has in mind? I have no idea, yet I'm confident I'll be safely kept until my work is done. At the end of my productive life, I'll be lovingly retired to a home created just for me. Even then, our relationship will continue.

Live in the Present

Is Bo concerned about why I teach him to softly assume different body frames; right posture then left, left posture then right, half-pass, shoulder in? Does he ask why? No. Which is a primary reason why he, like so many other wonderful horses, is amazing. How many people are obedient without asking why or sulling up until they reach agreement with the program? How many horses?

Our job is to learn what God has for us today, not crying over what we missed yesterday or worrying about tomorrow may bring. We are to be obedient, to softly and happily yield to His pressure. Let Him lead. It's silly, and perhaps self-destructive to the process itself, to worry about what each lesson means. Bo doesn't understand the plans I have for his future. Neither can we grasp what God's plan for each of us.

Knowing how to learn, I'm content in the daily process. Some tasks are more difficult to learn than others. I keep trying until the puzzles are solved. Accumulating ten thousand hours of deliberate practice is a marathon, not a sprint. I'm dedicated to the pursuit of excellence. If you faithfully practice every day, one day you will be exceptional.

Bo knows I will groom him at the end of every lesson, rubbing any muscle overly taxed while he worked through his exercise. I'll leave him snug and comfortable in his stall or turned out in the warm sunshine of the pasture to nibble grass or nap. At day's end, I know the Lord takes the watch as I snuggle under my covers without a care. I know He does not sleep.

"Be still and know that I am God."

Good night, Father. Good night, Bo.

IT'S THE RELATIONSHIP, NOT THE HORSE

If you love Me, you will keep my commandments. ~ John 14:15

A beautiful saint may be a hindrance if he does not present Jesus Christ, but only what Christ has done for him; he will leave the impression—"What a fine character that man is!"—that is not being a true friend of the Bridegroom (John 3:29). We have to be more careful of our moral and vital relationship to Him than of any other thing, even of obedience. ~ Oswald Chambers

Folks often say to Baber or me, "If only I had a horse like Bo. You're so lucky." Others ask if he's for sale. They want what I have. The truth is they don't want Bo per se; they want a relationship with their horse like I have with Bo. Just as it's wrong to admire the character of the beautiful saint Chambers refers to instead of Jesus Christ who initiated and directed their relationship. It's also wrong to see Bo as the special thing desired. What people want is the relationship I initiated and directed with Bo, made special by the commitment he also made.

Have you ever seen a father and son so obviously connected to each other that you wished you had a father like him or that your son would be like this one? Perhaps you thought, *How different life would be if I had a parent like that one.*

111

Remember that long-married couples still holding hands after fifty years of laughter and heartbreak, so obviously in love with each other that the line between them is a blur? Do you wish you were blessed with a husband like him or a wife like her? How lucky they are. *Why wasn't I as fortunate?*

It's easier for parents and their children to build strong bonds when they were blessed with great role models. If your parents taught you how to be both humble and strong, you have far better odds of successfully raising your own children. When you yearn for a perfect spouse, wonderful children, or a horse like Bo, what you long for isn't the person or the horse, but the special relationship they share.

The basics of building special relationship between horse and trainer also apply to relationships with children, spouses, friends, between teachers and their students, and any other relationship you pursue. You're more able to appreciate the possibilities of great relationships by observing the remarkable relationships others share. The most important relationship, of course, which serves as the cornerstone of all others, is your relationship with Jesus Christ.

Lessons in Leadership

Relationships aren't simple. Concepts that apply to relationships are like many others learned throughout our lifetimes. They're mysteries until the light bulb of understanding begins to glow. Where do we find the right partners for relationships? How do we build proper and strong foundations? How do we move from concentration on stuff and self and focusing steadfastly on Jesus? Like others, the journey begins with the first step. Matthew chapter 6 is a great primer for beginners and a wonderful reminder for those well into the relationship process.

In Matthew 6, Jesus lists a wonderfully objective list of behaviors we should do and behaviors we shouldn't. Jesus provides masterful lessons in charity and hypocrisy, showing how charitable deeds done before men have their reward here and now, earning no future reward from our Father in heaven. Verse 3 in chapter 6, is one of those mysteries we begin to unravel when our relationship with Jesus grows and matures.

But when you do a charitable deed, do not let your left hand know what your right hand is doing. ~ Matthew 6:3

A relationship with God has prerequisites like those encounter in higher education. Students can't understand complex material without learning the basics and building a foundation of knowledge first. Consider technology. Without the relevant foundation, it's pointless teaching me to construct a computer-generated holographic image when it took me two and a half hours and a phone call to the manufacturer to install my wireless mouse. (True story.) Talk technology and my eyes glaze over.

How do we build foundation and grow our relationship with Jesus Christ? Through His Word. How are we to pray? The Lord's Prayer is found in the sixth chapter of Matthew. When all else fails, this prayer covers every issue you'll encounter in life. Are you concerned that you just aren't prepared, that you don't have enough foundation? In this same chapter, Jesus also talks about the futility of worry. To consider the process of building a right relationship with God, I encourage you to concentrate on Jesus' lessons in Matthew 6.

As you progress in relationship you begin to understand why concentration on anything other than the relationship itself is a distraction. You will begin to understand Matthew 6:3, when your actions are generated by the relationship you share with Jesus Christ and not by conscious thought, debate, or intent. The charitable deed described in verse 3 is done unconsciously, just like breathing.

It is an automatic reaction, not a calculated deed. The doing of charitable deeds becomes so familiar that we don't realize we've even done one. We start with building habits of task, progressing until the mastery of tasks is replaced with the habit of obedience. When habit of obedience is reached, the limit of what is possible in a relationship expands to presently unknowable levels.

The relationship I have with Bo, when noticed by other horse owners, gets us talking shop. Those conversations are my best opportunity to influence the future success of the relationship the inquiring horse owner has with his or her own horse. The benefit of sharing my relationship testimony using words alone pales in comparison to seeing the benefits walked out with me and Bo.

The most important step in sharing my story is the awareness and following inquiry of the observer. The cliché, "a picture is worth a thousand words," is true for testimony. What is seen makes a bigger impact than what is preached. What people see in us must always live up to what we preach.

Until I learned this lesson, I had no idea how to present Christ to another person. It seemed all the other Christians knew how to share. I didn't. My grays are the key to my understanding that all I need do is present the truth of chosen relationship when seekers inquire. I've done that for years with people hoping for better results with their horses. Nothing about me causes someone to ask about the source of my security, joy, peace, and success. It's not *my* security, joy, peace, or success they want. What they want is their own relationship with Jesus Christ. Bo is not special in any way their horse is not. I'm not special in any way they are not. What is special is the relationship I share with Bo and my relationship with Jesus.

No great relationships happen by accident or luck.

Who most positively influenced your life? Was it someone standing on a stage giving you a laundry list of things to do? Did you get your money's worth from that expensive set of tapes telling you how to achieve happiness or wealth with little to no effort? Or have you been most greatly blessed by authentic people with simple talk, mannerisms, and message?

Once-in-a-Lifetime Relationships

Is there only one perfect horse in a lifetime? I don't think so. The method for producing seemingly once-in-a-lifetime relationships is formulaic. When the right trainer and horse get together, relationship still requires commitment, time, maintenance, leadership, obedience, correction, and confidence. Once trainers are properly educated and experienced, they may only have enough time and energy left in their careers to forge just one such relationship. These relationships take years to develop and mature, just like the marvelous relationship of that long-married couple mentioned at the beginning of this chapter.

Not surprisingly, great horse trainers usually make their living training horses. Every morning begins riding client horses and continues through the day until the work is done. Trainers often ride more than ten head per day, sometimes many more. Assistant trainers or apprentices work beginners until each horse reaches a stage where only the trainer can refine and advance the horse's level of performance. Little time remains to build relationships with a trainer's own horses. The horse trainer's business is to train and sell, train and sell.

There were years I looked forward to brushing a tail or cleaning a stall. All "my" horses had a closer personal relationship with my assistant trainer than they did with me. Rodolfo groomed them, bathed them, talked with them, and usually emptied the feed buckets into their stall feeders. The

115

horses didn't know (and didn't care) that I personally prepared each bucket, changing the content and quantity daily if needed. During the working day, Rodolfo handed me a horse and I taught the lesson. Afterwards, I handed the horse back to Rodolfo and started the next. Was I a good leader? I certainly tried. Was I building relationship? Yes, but not like I have with my grays today.

It's obvious that I believe in relationships. I have some natural ability as a horse trainer, but the desire, the heart, the relationship I built with each horse in my training barn is what allows me to do my best work. There were times I wondered why I didn't have the degree of success with all horses that I had with some. I usually knew what response I would get from each horse in competition. However, there were other horses I only had a good idea of what they would likely do. Consistency was not king. The difference between confidence and hopefulness is relationship.

No Time = No Relationship

Relationships thrive on commitment. Close relationships require time spent together. If I don't spend time with Bo and Swizzle nearly every day, other relationships will become more important. Those other relationships will strengthen as ours weakens. If all their time is spent with the herd, or simply with each other, my role diminishes. Bo and Swizzle will get what they need elsewhere.

The same is true in relationship with Jesus Christ. He is faithful to the demands of daily relationship. Are you? Is seeking Him a daily priority? If not, relationships with friends, family, video games, will strengthen as the one with Him weakens. Relationships take time. In the 1970s and '80s it became popular for parents to excuse the lack of quality time with their children by spending *quality* time with them. How misguided. Quality time is a judgment of worth, not a time frame. It's a misuse of the term itself and an exercise in rationalization to use the phrase *quality time* to describe short, content-laden time rather than time teaching or reinforcing relationship foundations of task, confidence, and affection.

The wet saddle blanket is a great method for making great horses. There's an old joke about a greenhorn rider advised to use this technique to gentle his unruly horse. Days later the greenhorn returned to the old hand and said, "I got that old saddle blanket plumb dripping before I put it on old Brownie—it didn't help at all." Of course, a wet saddle blanket is one that starts out nice and dry but gets saturated with horse sweat during long working sessions. Repeating the wet saddle blanket exercise makes great horses. Trying to cheat the required time commitment reduces the probability of building strong relationship. The only way to define quality time is by its fruit - the result of time spent together. True quality time produces stronger relationships. The greater the quality and quantity of time, the greater the strength of the relationship.

Are short periods of time spent with horses, children, or Jesus Christ ever meaningful? Absolutely. But they only when they reinforce what was previously established during longer periods of time spent together building a relationship.

Strangers in the House

Many parents today are shocked when they discover what their children do with their time. You hear stories on the nightly news documenting the often-tragic results of a parent-child relationship that left the kids adrift in the world without supervision, values, limits, or security. If truly committed to relationship with their children, parents wouldn't be surprised to find them involved in robbery, sex games, drugs, or worse. Such parents may be exhausted from work, housekeeping, friendships, athletic pursuits, school, whatever - maybe church activities. If you spend most of your parental time organizing and managing your children's

117

schedule, watch out. You're no longer mom or dad; you're the kid's activities coordinator. You sacrificed relationship with your children, creating a situation where the kids have no choice but to build other relationships outside the family.

There is no substitute in strong, secure relationships for time spent together. Bi-coastal marriages generally fail because all the important relationships exclude the spouse. You can't have a great marriage unless it's the one relationship that receives more of your concentration than any other, save your relationship with God. Your children are little more than resident strangers unless they spend a significant amount of time with you. You won't have the relationship you desire with Jesus Christ without making the attendant time commitment.

Once established, important relationships require ongoing maintenance. Relationships with other people require as much, or more, maintenance than the one you share with our horse. The quantity of time spent in relationship defines the quality of the relationship. You're free to think otherwise, but an objective evaluation of where you spend your time and the fruits of each relationship tell the real story.

Maintenance interludes can be short. Some days I hop on Bo or Swizzle bareback with a halter to play walk-trot trail. We do lots of standing around; I lie down on their backs to watch clouds drift across the sky; I hug their necks; we fortify our relationships. By sandwiching a few maneuvers between affection sessions, I reinforce the habit of obedience, something already mastered.

Never introduce something new with limited time. Rushing out for a twenty-minute drill on your horse triggers an unwritten law that requires your horse to contradict you or become confused. When that happens, your only responsible choice is to work through the issue until it's resolved. Your twenty-minute quickie drill becomes an hour and a half lesson.

When even a bareback ride isn't possible, I take a few moments to brush, pet, hug, and maybe offer a cookie. I feed cookies and carrots occasionally. Carrots are usually reserved for birthdays and trailer rides to ensure the horses get adequate hydration. Carrots contain lots of water, making them a good on hot days or when the horses are tied to the trailer at events.

Elements of Relationship

These quick visits may be considered quality time. However, they're only effective if used infrequently. Quality time spent with Bo and Swizzle adds to our relationship savings account. Time apart makes withdrawals. Short maintenance visits don't change the balance in the account one way or the other, but only for that one day. Unless I make significant regular deposits to our relationship accounts the balance begins to decline.

Relationship security comes from clarity, consistency, transparency, and accountability. Roles and rules must be crystal clear. Rules and boundaries are fixed and never violated without consequence. Consistency is arguably the most important component of relationship, though none of these elements are effective in the absence of the others. Roles, actions, and consequences must all be transparent. Equally true between people, relationship with horses demands easily understood directions and expectations. Otherwise the horse becomes confused, inconsistent in response, and insecure in the relationship.

Accountability is an aspect of relationships seen less frequently in western societies. Fewer great trainer-horse relationships exist, fewer great marriages exist, fewer great children are being raised, and fewer proper relationships between God and men exist today.

This lack of accountability is one of the greatest contributing factors to weak or failed relationships. When accountability is absent, we become insecure. The result is poor self-esteem. What's the motivation to behave if we're not held accountable for our decisions and behavior? Bad behavior in horses isn't disciplined because the responsible humans doesn't understand horse language or recognize rude, and potentially dangerous, behavior. The only other possibility is they don't care enough to do the work necessary to provide consistent leadership. The result is the same; either the horse or human is injured or the horse condemned, discarded or passed on to someone else. Do you see the similarity with many of today's youth?

People are no longer held accountable. Small wonder so many relationships, economies, and governments fail. Businesses and individuals don't live up to their advertising, promises, or responsibilities. There is no consequence for lack of performance. Do you think our relationship with God is the exception to this absence of accountability? It is not. We may attempt to rationalize our way out of the responsibility for poor decision-making or shift the blame to someone else (all the rage today), but God still holds us accountable. God is not mocked. He is not fooled. We can ride the lies we tell ourselves all the way to a final disastrous destination.

Belief Doesn't Equal Truth

Sometimes truth hurts. There's no pleasant way to describe sin. Calling sin a bad choice is another way of saying, "Give me a pass." Some will buy this line. I guarantee God will not. You are accountable. Consider fifteenth century explorers who believed the world was flat. All those names we learned in junior-high history and geography agreed the world was flat; all the maps agreed. No matter how strong their belief or widespread the agreement, the earth was not flat. Last I checked, it still isn't.

What's true is true. Holding a belief to the contrary is error. Greater belief or agreement won't make what is not true any less false. If you need a reality check regarding accountability, work with horses. Horses give you completely honest feedback about your behavior. They don't accept rationalization. If you don't offer true leadership and the responsibility that goes with it, horses will ignore you, hurt you, or leave you if given the opportunity. People selling the fallacy of equality without accountability are either misguided or liars; in either case, they would be complete failures as horse trainers.

Some horses put up with more bad behavior from humans than others, but eventually they all have enough of irritating humans and do whatever it takes to leave the scene or physically challenge the human. I usually take the horse's side, of course. Horses don't make excuses. They accept that there are horses lower on the pecking order and higher on the pecking order. A horse that earns a herd leadership accepts responsibility. Lead horse that fail to be accountable lose their leadership position and the herd itself may be placed in danger. Isn't it odd how horses often appear to be more insightful (and scriptural) than people?

Bo and Swizzle expect my requests or instructions to be clear and consistent. If they aren't, I failed to lead. Leaders deserve followership. When my horse gives me an incorrect response to a request, I always act. If the horse is unable to comply, it's my job to make him able. If the horse is unwilling to comply, I am ready to provide motivation. Horses are as accountable for making wrong choices as I am. The choice a horse makes and the reason he made it, determines the action I take in response.

Think about your relationships. The ones you value most are those where you understand your role; you are confident in the consistency of response from the one you relate to, and you know you'll be held accountable if you fail to hold up

121

your end. As trust, security, and affection build within a relationship, it moves from acquaintance to friendship, and perhaps more. God is faithful. God never changes. God is consistent. We have total confidence and security in His instruction and evaluation of us. His Word is clear, consistent, and transparent. He requires obedience and we are accountable to Him—just as we are accountable to one another.

LOVE AND LOVING LEADERSHIP

Love is patient…it rejoices in the truth. Love never fails. When I became a man, I put away childish things. ~ 1 Corinthians 13:4, 6, 8, 11

In the New Testament, love is more a verb than a noun. It has more to do with acting than with feeling. The call to love is not so much a call to a certain state of feeling as it is to a quality of action. ~ Dr. R.C. Sproul

Scriptural messages are always ones of relationship. At issue is right relationship to God the Father, Jesus Christ the Son, and the Holy Spirit. My message throughout this collection is about relationship with your horse and what it teaches you about relationship with God.

Bo and Swizzle were prey animals, alert and fearful of sudden movements or unexpected noises. Their relationship to me, and their confidence in my ability as a leader, produced a change in their nature. If our relationships remain clear and strong, Bo and Swizzle may eventually be fearless as leadership and relationship guides their new natures.

Christians should be on the path to fearlessness. It is evidence of right relationship with Jesus Christ. As faith in

123

almighty God grows, we eventually fear nothing and no one. Can the release from fear be achieved by affection alone - even love? Your own experience proves otherwise. Did your parents love you? If so, are you completely without fear? No, you aren't. If you're married, does your spouse love you unconditionally? Praise God if you can truthfully answer yes, but are you completely without fear? No, you aren't.

Is Jesus Christ your personal Savior? Are you a chosen child of the God of the Bible? If you answered yes to these questions, you are on a journey of relationship that will eventually remove all fear and worry from your life.

My Daddy's Bigger Than Yours

In their innocence, young children may be devoid of fear because of absolute confidence in the omnipotence of their parents. The young boy tells his neighborhood bully, "My daddy's bigger than your daddy." He has no fear because he believes his father is the biggest and greatest of all humans, without flaw or blemish.

Horses seldom progress in their emotional development and discernment past the level of prepubescent children. Many horses never make it out of the terrible twos. Until the little boy discovers his father is just a human with feet of clay, he retains faith in the total excellence of his daddy. Eventually every parent topples from the pedestal their children place them upon. As the little boy matures, he realizes that Dad is just a man, regardless of how much love there is between father and son. The young man learns fear when he sees the world and other humans with greater vision and awareness.

My goal with Bo and Swizzle is to continue adding to the breadth and height of the pedestal I told them I stand on. In the beginning, I proved I was on a pedestal, but only an inch above the ground. The surface of that first pedestal was small - just big enough for my personal space. One of the first lessons I teach horses is to only come within touching distance by invitation. I pet and hug them, but horses should not initiate contact. Respect the pedestal.

As days, weeks, and years pass, the pedestal grows in direct correlation to the depth and breadth of the relationship that exists between the horse and me. The physical space doesn't increase, but I earn greater respect and trust as the height of my pedestal rises.

Once we come to faith that our God is the only God, the almighty God, the God who spoke the world into existence, and the God who can do what he says he can, our respect and trust grows. Armed with this faith and relationship with our Lord, fear evaporates. God is a father bigger than any other. He will never fall from his throne and his feet aren't made of clay.

Many horse owners enjoy wonderful, loving relationships with their horses. Their horses are comfortable with touch; their horses are willing, eager, participants in the relationship. The horses may hold their humans in high esteem, seeking out and finding real pleasure in their company. All may be well until the horse becomes afraid, or until the owner exhibits fear.

Your horse may love you, but as an equal. That's great until trouble arrives. Many people are injured by adoring horses. In normal circumstances this friendly horse would never cause its owner injury. The horse may even love the human. But when fear takes over, the flight instinct kicks in and that half-ton of muscle and bone will be on the move. Many beloved owners were trampled in moments of panic.

Who Do You Run to?

When an owner is firmly established on a leadership pedestal, her horse won't default to fear mode. Right relationship with the trainer changes the horse's nature. When unsure about a sound, movement, or situation the horse immediately focuses on the trainer, looking for signs of uncertainty or fear. Finding neither, the horse asks, "What's the plan?" Trainers deserving the leadership pedestal they claim have a plan ready and provide direction or assurance as the situation warrants. Horses in strong relationship to their trainer, when confronted by fear, run *to* their trainer, not away.

Christians are also blessed with a new nature. Things that create fear and concern in most people are noted by Christians. Christians, however, do not default to fear. We look to God's throne for signs of uncertainty or indecision. There is none. Like a horse with faith in a worthy leader, the Christian will ask for direction or bask in the complete assurance that God has a plan at the ready. His plan is perfect, and we are safe. When in doubt, Christians run to Jesus for safety.

Love may be grand, but loving leadership creates confidence, strength, and defines our character. It allows us to enjoy perfect green pastures beside still, beautiful waters without concern for dangers lurking on the other side of the hill. God is on His throne. He told us he is God. He's proven he is God. We are secure.

What a wonder of grace is the gift of right relationship with Jesus Christ. What a wonder of grace is relationship with my grays.

YOU CAN'T FOOL GOD

O Lord, you have searched me and know me. For there is not one word on my tongue, but behold, O Lord, you know it altogether." ~ Psalm 139: 1, 3

Conscience is that faculty in me which attaches itself to the highest that I know, and tells me what the highest I know demands that I do. It is the eye of the soul which looks out either toward God or toward what it regards as the highest, and therefore conscience records differently in different people. ~ Oswald Chambers

Are you obedient? Is anything in the Bible create resistance the instant you read it? Such reactions are normal, and proof that we still respond to the matter carnally, not spiritually. We deceive ourselves when we avoid issues knowing they must still be conquered or resolved. These are areas in which we are disobedient. We don't follow the Lord's lead. The reason is not inability, though many offer that excuse. The reason is unwillingness. Pure and simple, we choose not to obey.

As the crafty humans we are, we avoid difficult issues by pretending they don't exist. If we never open the door, who could know that we would refuse to walk through? Let me show you what happens in a similar scenario from the trainer-horse perspective.

Some trainers avoid putting themselves and their horses in positions where they know the horse will refuse to comply with their request. Consider a horse that has a hissy fit when a rider touches it with a spur. We're not talking about the normal reaction a horse may have when first introduced to the spur that, if done correctly, is mild, of short duration, and is quickly followed by acceptance and understanding. Used properly, spurs are tools of refined communication.

Spurs should never be used in anger or frustration. It isn't unusual to hear riders say their horse won't accept a spur so they don't use them. I've ridden horses that didn't particularly care for spurs and some so responsive to small cues that spurs had no purpose. However, I never let a horse tell me I could not use a spur. That would admit there was a door I was afraid to open. Leaving that door closed, avoiding or pretending it isn't there proves leadership failure; where the led becomes the leader. That's the beginning of a bigger wreck waiting somewhere down the road.

When a Christian purposefully avoids that one truth in the Bible that causes him to sull up in stubborn defiance or just plain pissiness, it really a grab for the leadership role. God won't yield the day. He is too faithful. He knows that letting us have our way only leads to a bigger wreck on another day.

What to do when your horse tells you, "I don't do spurs!"

First you must be certain the case is one of refusal (unwillingness) and not inability due to poor foundation or lack of understanding. If the horse is unable to comply the good trainer will supply the foundation or education to make it able.

If the horse in unwilling, the trainer must determine the cause and find a way to create willingness. Trainers often have no idea what a horse experienced in the past that produced the problem behavior or reaction they face today. If the trainer knows why the horse refused it may be easier to create a plan for change. But knowing the why isn't necessary. The behavior or refusal is usually fixable regardless of its origin.

Christians are subject to the same issue. Are we unwilling or unable to walk through a door we've been avoiding? The only way to get the answer is to walk up to the door, open it, and attempt to walk through. If a horse tells me that bad things will happen if I attempt to use a spur, I guarantee I will open the door and try to go through.

But I won't approach the door without a carefully prepared lesson plan. Before addressing the spur issue, I would design basic exercises to establish a relevant dialogue.

My training method is built on a three-step system of communication. The method is the same for most problems. I'm using spurs to illustrate of the concept.

Suggest. Request. Insist.

This is my simple 3-step rule. First I suggest a response to the horse. If the suggestion doesn't produce the desired reaction I specifically ask the horse to comply with my direction. If the direct request doesn't work I must figure out the reason for failure. Was the horse unable or unwilling? If the horse is unable to respond appropriately I provide additional instruction until it is able. If the horse is unwilling, I go to the third step: I *insist* the horse do as I ask.

Here's the 3-step method from a mother and son point of view. One afternoon Mom walks into the living room to find her teenage son sprawled on the sofa playing video games. On her way down the hall she can't miss how messy his room is. Mom's wants her son to clean his room. She suggests, "I noticed your room needs to be straightened up." She looks at him – their eyes meet. Message delivered; Mom continues on her way.

Fifteen minutes later Mom comes back to the living room. Her son's feet haven't moved. Her suggestion didn't work. She makes a direct request, "Please go clean your room." Again, eyes meet in understanding but the kid doesn't get off the couch. The request failed.

Nothing prevents the boy from getting up. Mom escalates to the third step – she insists. She knows exactly what's needed to get the kid up and start feet moving swiftly in the direction of his room. Having been consistently "trained", the son realizes nothing else in life is going to happen until he cleans his room.

The key is consistency. On most occasions the son would immediately move his feet and go clean his room at his mother's suggestion alone. Relationship isn't static, training is never cast in stone, and Mom's faithfulness to step in when needed maintains her son's level of obedience.

Training a horse also requires consistency, faithfulness, and following through the entire 3-step process until feet move - every single time.

Once I establish a leadership position with the horse, however tenuous, I increase the difficulty of maneuvers we perform until the horse is confident that I'm fair and capable of leading. Once past this point, I use the spur to ask for a maneuver the horse just performed. I'm introducing the spur as a form of communication, not anything new. I want to see how the horse reacts to the spur within a very structured context. I'm using the scientific method to diagnose the situation. Since only one variable changed from the maneuver we just did well I know that any resistance on the horse's part is a result of the difference. In this case, the variable that changed was the addition of the spur.

With any training issue, whether between God and man or trainer and horse, there must be a plan. God's plan is always relevant, proper, and perfect. There is no response we can make to His pressure or communication that He isn't already three steps ahead of us. He knows the range of possible reactions we might give and is prepared in advance to respond instantly with His next move. I call this "The Dance." He leads, we respond. Depending on our response, He leads again. And so it continues.

Take Smaller Steps

If we determine that the issue isn't "I can't" but "I won't!" the worthy trainer will break down the door of unwillingness. A trainer could pretend that the door isn't there, but the horse won't be fooled and the relationship will be damaged. Refusing to approach a problem or pretend it isn't there is playacting; trying to sell our refusal as innocence rather than disobedience. You can't fool God. Attempting it proves we are the fools.

How do we help a horse that won't willingly accept the touch of a spur? As with any horse or human training program, we break down the process into the simplest possible steps. If we encounter resistance at any point there is always a smaller step possible. The process of breaking a task down into steps is like the math theorem - between any two points there is always another point.

Let's begin working through the spur issue with a very basic step. From the ground, using a rope halter and lead, work the horse through a variety of bending and yielding exercises. This process establishes the foundation for horses that are easy to halter. By mastering these exercises, horses learn respect, trust, confidence, accountability, and obedience. Next, I'd consider rubbing the horse from nose to tail with a stiff riding crop. If you can't do these little exercises quickly and quietly don't attempt addressing the actual

Dancing - pressure, yield, pressure, yield - lightly place the butt end of the crop handle on the horse's side where the spur normally touches, and ask him to move away from the pressure. Patience is the most important tool trainers have. If the horse leans into the handle of the crop (and at first, they all do), continue to hold it firmly. Don't press harder! Be consistent and light. As soon as the horse even thinks about moving away, release the pressure by taking the crop from the horse's side. Timing is everything.

Rub the horse a few times with the crop on the withers and croup to show the horse that the crop itself has no power of its own. When the horse is calm and quiet I'll apply pressure to the horse's side again. Repeat this sequence until the horse moves away easily and lightly as the crop handle touches his side. Then do the other side. We're trying to determine the source of the negative reaction to spur pressure. Where is it triggered? Eventually the horse will accept the pressure on his side and move softly away. This is the precise response we want from a spur.

Build Confidence

Once the groundwork is successfully completed it's time to mount up and systematically work through the door of resistance. The process is the same. Back to basics; suggest, request, and insist on soft obedience. Begin with an easy exercise, perhaps a figure eight at the walk. Show the horse the pattern and work through it several times until the horse knows exactly what is expected. This is how we build the horse's confidence. We let him win.

Change the posture (frame) of the horse and continue the figure eight at an easy jog. Use seat and leg aids to transition from one direction to the other. If the horse isn't happy with the increase in speed return to the walk and begin again.

132

Reins are used only when necessary, offering the horse a hint that his response isn't quite right. Once the horse responds lightly to leg pressure in the circles and through the middle of the figure, add the spur. Leg pressure is reduced when the spur touches the horse's side. The spur doesn't add pressure, it replaces pressure the leg was applying. If we do our job well, the horse will perform correctly without concern for the spur.

This starts to clear the mess that blocked the door. By working a plan patiently, wisely, and consistently, the trainer and horse build confidence in one other and strengthen the relationship already in place.

Whenever you leave a hole in the foundational training of a horse it will always come back to bite you later, and never at a convenient time. Sooner or later the deficit will prevent you from acquiring a higher skill or limit the level of obedience and confidence your horse is able to offer. No issue is repaired or resolved by ignoring it. The work must be done. Good trainers know this. You won't fool the horse.

Is God fooled when we try to ignore that one thing we're unwilling to admit? We only deceive ourselves. The work must be done sooner or later. The door must be opened. We won't get a pass; the bill will become due and payable. It's easier to learn our lessons in a natural order of progression than wait until a foundational weakness shows up at the worst possible moment. Where are you unwilling? Where do you think you're fooling God -- or yourself?

FAITH AND EFFORT

Ask, and it will be given to you; seek, and you will find; knock, and it will be opened to you. ~ Matthew 7:7

God created the world out of nothing; so long as we are nothing, he can make something out of us. ~ Martin Luther

My mother told me from the time I was little that I could be, or do, anything I desired if I just wanted, worked, and tried hard enough. I don't remember if the work part was included in her guarantee, but I'll give her the benefit of my doubt. She passed away fourteen years ago, so I can't pick up the phone and ask her.

Was my mother right or wrong?

Scripture tells us we can move mountains with faith as a mustard seed (Matthew 17:20). Jesus told his disciples that anything they asked in His name would be granted to them (John 14:14).

Is Scripture right or wrong?

With all that I was and had, including the lessons my mother taught me, I figured God had given me all I needed to be able to succeed in any endeavor I "really worked for" as I served Him. In my first two decades of life I admit that the service aspect of my relationship with the Lord was probably not as high on my daily to-do list as it should have been. However, I never felt removed from God - even during one period of complete rebellion when I mistakenly believed that God categorically failed me.

My genetics provided an athletic body, enough intelligence to be accepted into membership in Mensa (an organization for folks with an IQ in the top 2 percent of the population), thick red hair, navy blue eyes, and a peaches-and-cream complexion. After making the late childhood move from the shy, frumpy, analytical girl I had been to the slim, chic, and extroverted teen I became, I thought I had the world by the tail on a downhill drag.

There was the little complication of my dysfunctional family, but who among us had Ward and June Cleaver as parents?

It seemed to me that the assets I brought to the game of life should be sufficient to provide me with the ability and responsibility to establish, direct, and succeed in the life goals I chose. I figured God had already done His share of the work by blessing me with what came naturally. The rest was up to me. I don't mean that I thought I was so wonderful that I only had to announce myself to the world and I would succeed. My belief was more that I had no excuses of extreme poverty, physical handicap, or mental weakness to cut myself any slack. Anything less than success was pure failure.

High expectations were the norm in our household. I got my first A- in sixth grade. Until then I earned all A's. The A- was such a failure in my parents' estimation they grounded me until the next report card came out six weeks later.

Hindsight being what it is, I was not as well-adjusted as I thought, evidenced by many self-destructive moments occurring in my early adulthood. God never let me go down any of those dark roads so far that I couldn't return to the light. I racked up life lesson after life lesson. A philosophy I still believe is that mistakes happen. They just shouldn't be stupid ones. I consider making a mistake twice totally unacceptable. (The rule only applies to me, so don't worry about the horses.) I can't think of any mistake I repeated, but I guarantee I had no problem finding new and more creative ones to make.

Life went on. My life education continued. I learned some very valuable lessons being the wife of a violent alcoholic. Suffice it to say that the Lord used this experience to prepare me for what He had in mind for later. I am forever grateful for all the difficult times. Without them I wouldn't know the Serenity Prayer and, more importantly, learned to live by it. The most valuable insights we gain often come with the pain of experience. There is no greater blessing than a spirit of gratitude, whether received as a gift or learned the hard way.

Gratitude

There's a great deal of research and authorship available about gratitude. Gratitude is a wonderful thing. Gratitude engenders generosity. The things that matter most in life don't diminish when you give them away, they increase. Gratitude, like love and education, is one of these things. Are we born knowing how to be grateful and content? Hardly. Do little children share with others because they come hardwired that way? No, they must be taught to share.

Few people talk about contentment anymore. Most people today are concerned with passion. They want to feel passionate about their jobs, relationships, and passionate about their sports and hobbies. Passion is wonderful, but even a right relationship with God isn't passionate all the time. Anything that burns passionately all the time burns itself out in no time.

"Too much" is the heart of discontent. When did enough become not enough? Ungrateful hearts breed bitterness and discontent. Practice gratitude. Pray with gratitude. The Lord is worthy and you'll feel better.

Decades ago, when the most significant relationship of my life ended I became a typical sinner in rebellion against God. Yet even in that moment of complete dejection I was grateful for experience that relationship provided. I believed the old saying is true, "It is better to have loved and lost than to never have loved at all."

It took nearly thirty years before I understood why that relationship had to end. The reason falls loosely under the category of idolatry. If that relationship continued, my eyes would have always gone first to his face and not to *His* face. In retrospect, I believe God would have brought me to the same place I am today no matter how that relationship affected me. I might have needed a correction more devastating than the break up felt. God never loses one of his chosen. Ever.

Let's return to what my mother taught me and what Scripture says about what we can do if we just try hard enough or have enough faith. Things went well in my career. Not quite in the normal progression, but nicely overall. I finished my college degree at night, working one or two jobs during the day. My usual story is that I lucked into management at age nineteen, but it's probably more accurate to say that God placed me in a management position at nineteen years of age.

So far it seemed my mother's instruction was right. If I worked hard enough I seemed able to accomplish any goal I set for myself. I wanted to be a self-employed business consultant. All the preparation that was necessary I achieved. For years I worked and played—but mostly worked. I was active in my church and blessed with great friends. I pursued my dreams. I ran a 5K, bought a motorcycle, and I loved my dachshund, Snooker.

Miracles Do Happen

A minor blip in the plan was a small accident that happened a few weeks before my twenty-fifth birthday that ruined my knees. My athletic dreams appeared to come to an end. I played church softball for a while, but the knees just couldn't cut it. There have been more than a few surgeries over the years and the knee situation alone taught me many lessons, revealing just how merciful and faithful the Lord is.

How so? I'll make this as short as possible so we can return to my actual topic. By the time I was thirty-two, I woke up each morning and evaluated my walking ability for the day. Would it be a crutch day, a cane day, or a day with no need for assistance? At times my restrictions were slightly irritating, but I often rode my motorcycle with crutches strapped to the sissy bar with bungee cords.

My knees were horrible. After riding a friend's horse for an hour, I couldn't walk. After dismounting (like a rag doll) I depended on the horse to be my crutch until I could stand again on my own. Doctors in Omaha declared me permanently partially disabled. I let that declaration go in one ear and out the other with no intermediate stops in between. My doctors instructed me to sit unless it was absolutely necessary to walk. They had to be kidding. I had way too much drive for that.

The next issue was Meniere's disease. I got so dizzy I dropped to the floor, rooted to the spot until the attack passed. Looking for an outlet for excess energy I tried flying small airplanes, but the dizzy thing ruled it out after one flying lesson. The next option on my list was getting a horse. Mind you, I'd never owned a horse before.

The Saturday after my first (and last) flying lesson I decided to buy a horse. By Sunday afternoon my new horse was safely tucked in at a local boarding stable. Even though I had no experience training horses at the time, I bought one who'd never been ridden. This is a typical greenhorn mistake, though in my case it was just part of the plan. I vividly remember a lesson my horse taught me about what spurs used in ignorance can lead to when the horse in question is already bucking. I never repeated that mistake. My first horse, and the ones that followed, were my first instructors as I learned to be a horse trainer.

Eventually, my wonderful God-provided husband (of twenty-five years now) and I moved to Phoenix where I became a full-time horse trainer and breeder. I know, I skipped a whole bunch of stuff getting from there to here, but I'm still trying to get back on point.

The year is 1990, and I'm now on a ranch north of Phoenix, pursuing my career as a breeder and horse trainer - with ruined knees. Miraculously, the Lord blessed me with twenty years of hauling hay bales and feed sacks, starting colts under saddle, training for the show pen as well as for customers who just wanted a safe horse, breeding and foaling out well over a hundred mares, even specializing in training stallions. In 1999, my orthopedic surgeon examined new X-rays of my knees (one more surgery being planned) and said, "You can't do what you tell me you do. It is not possible." Not only possible, but I continued for another nine years after that. My official training career ended twenty years after it began, almost to the day.

From Miracle to Heartbreak

So, what's my point? Was Mother correct when she told me I could be, or do, anything? In this case, yes. However, the story of my horse career includes a multitude of heartbreaking experiences my husband and I lived through during our time in Arizona. When we talked about our breeding program, our veterinarians and friends could only say, "If it wasn't for bad luck, you'd have no luck at all."

I'll never forget my friend, Jackie, laying across the hip of baby colt while I lay over his neck to keep him from struggling up onto a shattered front leg. He had the baby-soft hair that only knew sunlight and air for three weeks. This colt was one you wait for your whole life. Horse people in the area had been calling and coming to see this colt ever since he arrived. Our veterinarian spread the word about him to other clients and breeders. I already had one once-in-a-lifetime foal; this would have been my second. I guess that when something is truly once-in-a-lifetime there cannot be a second.

Jackie and I lay across the warm little foal, so beautiful and healthy—except for the fracture just below his left knee. The afternoon was fast becoming stormy. Angry clouds gathered and roiled in the sky as a storm rapidly approached. Though barely past midday, ominous dark clouds and howling winds blew desert sand and manure dust into our eyes. What an eerie, sad picture we must have made; the colt's mother standing over us, expecting us to fix her baby. Jackie, momma, the baby, and I waited for Dr. Rezzonico to arrive.

The colt's registration papers from the Appaloosa Horse Club arrived in the mail the same day he died. His registered name was the same as his famous AQHA daddy, *Kid Clu*.

My husband stayed in the house. He couldn't come out to witness the end of this foal and watch yet another dream die. Over the years we had many wonderful foals that didn't make it. I am grateful to have no regrets about any of them. We did everything right and humanly possible; it was just the luck of the draw - or so it seemed. We wondered if we were being punished, but for what? My walk with the Lord was getting closer and richer by the day. I know it was. Just as the darkest night comes just before the dawn, so it often is with God. He was determined to more finely focus my attention.

Remember, my mother taught me I could accomplish anything if I tried hard enough. I believed God had provided me with all the ability needed to take advantage of the opportunities presented. I never prayed for myself. Had I done so, I thought it would be a slap in God's face. It would be evidence that He hadn't fully prepared me, and how wrong could that be? My prayers were always for others. I suppose you can already see where I was going wrong.

John Lyons and his entourage came to our place to do his symposiums and private student tutoring, staying for nearly two weeks each time. One year Gary and Judy Jones of Lamesa, Texas, came to conduct Cowboy Church in our covered arena Sunday morning. The Jones parked their camper in front of our house and stayed an few extra days. What a blessing they were. We opened our hearts to them. Their witness gave me one of those light bulb moments. What was illuminated in a light so bright even I couldn't fail to see it was -- arrogance.

Arrogance

My belief in the ability and presumed responsibility for creating my every success was arrogance. I felt that I shouldn't need God daily since He'd equipped me to take care of myself. Wrong. He was faithful to give me failure after failure - yet without guilt - until I finally fell on my knees to confess that I'd reached my limit and could go no further on my own. When I say I went to my knees I mean literally, which for me was no small undertaking. I had no more ability or try to offer. I was spent out. There was nothing left.

The blessing came. God is faithful. He had increased the pressure on me consistently and incrementally until I reached the point where I gave. This is the same process we use to train horses. God, as the perfect leader, created the plan. He presses until we *must* move. The pressure disappears instantaneously, miraculously, when we are obedient.

Sometimes slight pressure may be applied again to test and reinforce a lesson. By yielding immediately, the pressure - tiny as it may be - disappears in an instant. If we didn't truly learn the lesson the pressure slowly builds again until we must move. Soon, even a hint of the now familiar pressure elicits God's desired response. It works the same way with horses. We begin using soft rein pressure to ask the horse to yield its head and neck. Pressure applied slowly, consistently, and incrementally builds until the horse gives to the rein. When the training process is complete, just the motion of our hand lifting results in the immediate, soft yielding of the horse's head and neck. No pressure at all. Just a hint, a suggestion, is all it takes.

The process is the same when God brings us into obedience. He is always perfect in His timing and precise in His cues, whereas we can never reach that perfection of leadership. Our timing will never be perfect, but, thankfully, horses forgive our minor deficiencies.

Who Sets the Goals?

Did I find my happy ending once the light bulb revealed my arrogance? No. I found a beginning. Everyone has conflicts between the goals we set for ourselves and the plans God has for us. At the beginning of each relationship with a horse I have a good idea what I hope to accomplish. The horse learns in bits and pieces, without understanding where our journey will take him. I see the big picture; the horse does not. My job is to bring the horse through our many lessons and build a relationship that will achieve the goal I originally planned.

We only see bits and pieces of the plan for our own lives. God alone knows the goal He has for each of us. In the end, guess whose plan will be accomplished?

There's a point where God bounces people who refuse to yield from the program. The same is true with horses. I've

143

only had a few outright failures that resulted in flunking a horse completely. Original goals may need revision as I learn more about a horse's personality, athletic limitations, or discover unexpected talents. Some horses you expect to work the rail love to jump. The experience of learning and revising goals is mine, not the horse's. I'm not omnipotent or anything like that, but I have enough expertise to evaluate untrained horses and form accurate opinions about what their highest and best use might be. Sometimes I'm wrong, and make appropriate adjustments as training progresses.

God is omnipotent. He knows what we can be. Does the fact that I have a good idea of what a horse can become mean it reaches its highest potential? No. Does God's knowing our potential mean we all reach it? Again, no. Horses brings input to the training process just as we do. Every horse has a degree to which he will yield and continue progressing in its lessons. So do we. Our free will determines how high we climb on our personal ladders of possibility. The degree to which we yield, commit to, and obey our trainer determines how long we remain in the progressive training process and relationship we enjoy with God.

There's always conflict when our plans don't coincide with God's. After that first light bulb went on I continued to feel pressure. At first it was minor and I wasn't motivated to make a substantial effort to find release. God initiated changes in our lives that brought us to Texas. Hindsight is 20/20. It's easy to connect the dots of God's handiwork in the rearview mirror. Few (if any) get a clear vision looking ahead. But God is gracious to provide understanding about our past.

God often revealed the error of my ways in hindsight, long after I corrected the problem. There was no stigma or grudge, nothing but greater understanding on my part and a recognition of grace on His. As Baber and I worked through ten years in Texas the pressure came and went with lessons

144

learned and deeper relationship with God. Every day I seek greater focus and abandonment to His plan and purpose.

My mother was right. I can do anything I work at hard enough—if it fits into God's plan for me. We waste so much energy on plans we'll never accomplish. If we keep eyes and ears tuned on our leader even while pursuing plans doomed to ultimate failure, He will be faithful to redirect our feet at the appropriate moment.

Horses learn by making mistakes. Unless I allow it to commit to a mistake, how can I let it know it made a wrong choice? As long as the horse's eyes, ears, and body are attentive to me, it will never receive anything more than a gentle correction to set its feet back on the correct path. My job is to present the lesson so the easiest response is the correct one. Only blatant rebellion receives harsher correction. I ask; the horse responds. As the horse's education advances, I must trust him to make good choices.

When a mistake is made, I gently put him back where I intended him to be. God prepares us over time, allowing us to make mistakes which He gently corrects. If we refuse and become stubborn - if we mutiny - His corrections can be harsh. Thank God when they are! Harsh corrections are proof positive that we're still in the program and God remains committed to our successful outcome.

When corrections cease, God is either letting us soak in our success or we've been bounced from His program. If that happens, people either stew around the back forty until He calls them home or they go where all rogue stock ends up.

Is it necessary to evaluate every desire we have against God's bigger plan? Not really. Some things we think we want are so ridiculous that we show ourselves to be fools to pursue them. Would it make any sense for a lame, definitely mature woman to dream of playing in the NFL? If I wanted it enough, if I tried hard enough, could I achieve that goal?

That plan deserves to be filed under stupid. Set your goals, take the steps necessary to achieve them, and trust God to reward or correct your actions. Remain focused on Him and all will be well.

What's possible in your life? With my knees, no one would have bet a dollar in 1988 that I would be spend twenty years training horses. Yet it happened. People can do what seems impossible. God gives us talents, abilities, and free will. Your resources will take you only so far if God has other plans, but there's no limit to what you can do if God approves your plans and equips you to succeed.

COMMUNICATION AND MAKING
MISTAKES

John the Baptist says, "I am not the Christ...He must increase, but I must decrease. ~ John 3:30

Watch for all you are worth until you hear the Bridegroom's voice in the life of another. Never mind what havoc it brings, what upsets, what crumblings of health, rejoice with divine hilarity when once His voice is heard. You may often see Jesus Christ wreck a life before He saves it. ~ Oswald Chambers

The peace on earth of the nativity is often misunderstood. "Glory to God in the highest, and on earth peace, goodwill toward men" (Luke 2:14).

This peace and goodwill referred isn't among or between men, but rather that the Christ, the Messiah, came to *allow* peace between a Holy God and sinful men. Earlier in life I thought this verse meant we were to behave peaceably with all mankind and that the goodwill mentioned was between one man and another. I was wrong. This message of peace and goodwill carries such great magnitude because it assures us we are redeemed and able to stand before a holy God.

Without sin or blemish, washed white as snow through the blood sacrifice of Jesus Christ.

Though goodwill and peace are available at each step in our journey, there's no guarantee the road will always be smooth and trouble free. If we are in a relationship with God we are in training, just as our horses are in training. The methods needed to get our attention may cause temporary discomfort or distress. Sometimes we must watch friends and loved ones go through trials as the Holy Spirit works through issues with them. We err if we interfere without invitation.

Just as Jesus Christ may often wreck a life before He saves it, the biggest horse training wrecks may occur just before achieving the greatest advancement in communication.

Communication is required before obedience is possible. As we discovered earlier, the only way to let a horse know it made the right decision is by *releasing* pressure. Good trainers allow the horse to commit to a mistake before correcting it. If horses are always kept just short of making an error, there will never be an opportunity to explain the error. Horses don't speak *human*; humans must learn to speak *horse*.

Animal activists and amateurs don't always understand the love and devotion good trainers apply in the training process. What may appear to an observer as unfair or too difficult may be the perfect means to move the horse toward confidence, obedience, and security.

Worthy trainers provide proper food, water, exercise, mental stimulation, leadership, safety, and security for horses that will ultimately change from the spirit of a prey animal to the spirit of relationship. Love and affection grow between the trainer and horse as the basics of task and obedience gradually transition to love and devotion. It is the same for human students who learn to love their teachers. The most admired and beloved teacher is never the one who gives easy A's. The most loved teacher is the one who instills

148

knowledge, concept, relationship, accountability, and confidence in the student. Think of the teachers you hold in the highest esteem, are they the teachers who nurtured the desire to achieve or gave everyone easy A's?

Who taught you to be confident?

If you don't understand how horses learn and relate I ask you to stay out of the relationship between trainer and horse. If you limit the good trainer's options to communicate, even when the immediate picture looks bad for the horse, you may jeopardize the horse's future. A wise man once said, "Don't judge what you don't understand."

I'm sure you know the saying, "The path to hell is paved with good intentions." Such clichés and sayings persist because they're based in truth. You may intend to save loved ones from pain or danger by interfering with their relationship with God. But your well-intentioned act may prevent God from doing what He intended rather than helping them. God must have free rein with His children to establish communication that builds relationship and eventual obedience.

Jesus never hollers and the Spirit only speaks in a still, small voice. I seldom raise my voice to either a horse or human. If they care, they listen. If your voice is louder than His, neither you nor your loved one can hear God's Word as intended. In this respect, the Lord is like a horse. The horse escalates its message bit by bit—but not verbally. Good trainers understand what horse body language means and catch what the horse is trying to tell them long before the horse explodes in bucking, kicking, or rearing. These extreme behaviors are best understood as screams of frustration or fear. If you don't catch the small communications God sends you, don't be surprised when He increases the pressure to get your attention.

I Missed the Signs

Have you ever heard of a horse that exploded with absolutely no warning? Few experienced trainers ever told such a story. It's exceedingly rare for a horse to display extreme behavior without giving plenty of notice. Most people just don't understand how horses communicate and are surprised when bad things happen.

Recently, I had a conversation with a friend, the father of one of my past students. He was riding his horse, a trustworthy well-broke mare. The mare unexpectedly came upon a llama, bolted, and threw him. Although he recovered from most of his injuries, he lives with chronic back pain. It's a sad situation. While he didn't hold the result of the accident against the mare, he sold her and may not ride again. As he walked me through the details of the incident it was clear the tragedy could have been avoided. The mare gave plenty of notice that she was in trouble and needed direction. Not finding it, she reverted to a prey animal's primary defensive mechanism: flight.

As we spoke, I asked if his mare had stopped. Yes, she had. I asked if she became stiff like a statue. Yes, she had. I asked if the mare lifted her head high into the air as she stared at the llama. Yes, she had. All these are predictable and routine methods of communication for a horse. Stopping abruptly is normal when a horse senses danger. Good trainers evaluate the situation and respond with leadership. If my friend understood what his mare tried to tell him while still reasonably calm, he could have acted to de-escalate her panic. He might have continued his ride that day and enjoyed future rides.

The mare gave my friend another opportunity to provide leadership. She became rigid, another normal response in the circumstances and another opportunity to change the outcome. At that point, she was still willing to be led. Leadership didn't come. The mare's next move was to throw her head up in the air to get the best possible view of the alien creature (llama). Even then there was still a chance to communicate, but he didn't know how.

In most panic situations, communication needs to happen quickly. There wasn't an opportunity for my friend to consider his options in a leisurely manner. Emergencies require experience, giving the right response without thinking about it. After running out of options, the mare gave up waiting for conversation and bolted. I was sad for both my friend and his nice little mare.

Attentive Christians know God intimately enough to know that some difficulties we face are the result of missing signs He provided. Like horses, God seldom delivers an explosive life event without giving warning signals in advance. Learn to recognize the small signals and signs before your horse, or God, must explode to get your attention.

Everyone knows someone who was fundamentally changed after surviving a life-and-death experience. This is an example of God using an explosion to get our attention. Those who "heard the Bridegroom's voice" are forever changed as a result. Those who wouldn't, or couldn't, hear His voice eventually returned to the place they were before experience. The life lesson, the opportunity to be transformed, was lost.

Without effective communication, lessons are only minimally successful. Students in some public schools where students who only understand Spanish are taught in English. Children of the inner-city may have a vastly different vocabulary from their suburban-raised teachers. The result of failed communication is ever-increasing drop-out rates.

Communication must be established before education is possible. Education must begin before obedience can be achieved. Obedience is the key to leader-follower relationships.

Do You Yield from Obedience or Pain?

Effective training works in one of two ways: (1) results are achieved when the student learns to yield to pain or (2) through obedience.

While some argue its efficacy, one can learn by yielding to pain. Such techniques produce stress-induced results. Torture is the ultimate illustration of yielding to pain. The other training method, yielding through obedience, builds a firm foundation upon which future lessons may be built.

Using pain as a learning tool may produce submission, but will never build relationship. Bits, spurs, gadgets or anything that inflicts pain on a horse is always wrong. Tools are useful. Pain is not.

Students who cram for exams for the sole purpose of getting the best grade possible don't retain much. Building a strong base wasn't their goal. The goal was a grade and not an education. I was a master-crammer in college. I'd outline the material, study it the night before an exam (even finals), and usually pass with an A. Do you think I retain much of that information today? Nope. This type of learning is like that from yielding to pain. The student wants to avoid the negative outcome a poor grade would cause so he works to get the best grade, not to learn the content of the lesson.

Cheating

Like human students, horses learn to cheat when they don't feel a significant relationship with the teacher - and they think they can get away with it. When allowed to, horses cheat by doing only what is necessary to make the pressure go away. No foundation is built. No security, leadership, trust, or confidence is established.

The relationship a student has with his or her teacher is the key. If I had great respect for an instructor I worked hard to gain his or her approval and master the lesson material. In a right relationship, the student wouldn't dream of cramming. It would show unacceptable disrespect for the teacher.

During my teens I was a figure skater. My pro (instructor) was tough. But I respected her and worked my tail off to do everything perfectly. The high I felt on those red-letter days when she made a positive comment provided ample motivation to keep me working.

I applied myself, progressed, and did quite well. Then my pro retired. I think I was the last non-family student she had. In came the new pro, a personable young woman with a great record. She was always positive and cheerful, even when my work was less than wonderful. There is no drive to excel when adequate is perfectly acceptable. I didn't respect the new pro because she didn't respect me enough to demand excellence.

Likewise, Christians who cheat the process of learning about and from God only harm themselves. If they yield only from fear they won't experience the possibilities the relationship being offered holds. No foundation is built and they don't receive the immediate benefits of His leadership; trust, security, and confidence. Some horse owners and trainers confuse cheating with success, errantly giving misplaced affection and rewards to their horse.

Research proves that we get more of what we reward. If we reward cheating, horses learn to be more creative and frequent cheaters. If we reward adequate, then we'll get more of the same. Trust me, both God and horses know the difference.

Abuse

Yes, parents, these principles also apply to children. You knew this was sounding way too familiar. Any biologically healthy adult human can become a father or mother, just like any person with access to a horse can call himself a trainer. It takes well-educated, dedicated, persistent, and obedient parents to properly raise a child. Likewise, it takes well-educated, dedicated, and persistent trainers to properly train a horse. The cause of most disobedient or dangerous teenagers is parents who were absent physically, emotionally, or both.

Worse, some kids have abusive parents. Children are vulnerable to abuse when otherwise well-intentioned parents lack the discipline and dedication to properly teach, defend, and love them. Horses suffer abuse when otherwise well-intentioned trainers are unable to properly teach, defend, and relate to a horse. What was that saying about good intentions and the path to hell?

We are responsible to teach children and horses to communicate. That means learning to listen. Building solid relationships is our responsibility as parents and horse trainers. It's easier to achieve proper relationships with horses and children if we're rightly related to God. He's the ultimate authority on right relationship.

Without God, there is no ultimate authority and example of how to build relationships. The best plan for success as a parent or horse trainer is to establish our own obedient relationship with God. He teaches us to communicate and build foundations for greater understanding in the future. Parents teach relationship and build strong foundations to last throughout a child's lifetime. Training horses is little different. Take advantage of your opportunity to learn from the Master trainer.

People who experience life-and-death issues, who yield from pain and not obedience, may follow the Lord for a time, only to return unchanged to their original errant path. Are their names truly in the Book of Life? We can't know God's ultimate plan for ourselves, much less anyone else. Just as yielding to pain in horses fails to produce a strong foundation, the same is true in humans who break under pressure without making the proper connection with God. Through pain, horses learn fear and hatred. So do humans.

The horse that will not yield except to pain is just as lost as the human who is unwilling to yield to great leadership.

God is faultless in training His children. Human parents and horse trainers make mistakes. All trainers make wrong judgments. It's important to realize that all error is not sin. My goal in life was to never make the same mistake twice. I keep making new ones because I keep trying. In right relationships, horses are very forgiving creatures. It's my responsibility to listen to the horse as much as it is the horse's to listen to me. Without communication, there is no education. Without communication, there is no relationship.

The more we work on relationship with our Master the more effective leaders we become in our families, our communities, our nation, and with our horses.

LEADERSHIP OR DOMINATION

Woe to those who make unjust laws, to those who issue oppressive decrees. ~ Isaiah 10:1

Wicked men obey from fear; good men from love. ~ Aristotle

Effective horse trainers use one of two methods to get the desired response from a horse: obedience (leadership) or domination. All trainers, as they work with ever-increasing numbers of horses, eventually encounter at least one horse that will not be obedient without first being dominated. Good trainer only resort to dominance when all reasonable attempts to offer leadership fail.

Escalation of power occurs naturally in the horse world. It's part of normal herd behavior. However, once a dominant horse establishes its superior position and the inferior horse submits, the overpowering behavior of the dominant horse reverts to relationship or herdship. The need to prove dominance disappears unless the lower order horse makes a conscious choice to challenge the dominant horse again. Only human nature persists in domination after the other has surrendered. It isn't the nature horses.

Sometimes a horse may be dominated by a freak circumstance. If the horse isn't injured this can be a fortuitous situation. A friend of mine in Arizona (almost a legend in his ability to turn out exceptional horses using consistent, quiet methods—he didn't even own a correction bit) shared the story of a rebellious stallion sent to him for training.

The stud was four years old and full of himself. He was an idiot to halter, didn't lead willingly, and was just rank. After being in my friend's barn for a few days, the stud was haltered and came out of his stall with his usual bad attitude. This day, however, the stallion slipped on the concrete breezeway aisle and fell. My friend had nothing to do with it, but as soon as the horse scrambled to his feet he had a completely different attitude. Somehow, the stud associated the trainer with being put on the ground. He was obedient thereafter.

A Pretty Problem

A few years ago, I took a mare in training that was pushy, nasty, resistant, and barely rideable at a walk when she arrived. Once were Lizzie's issues fixed I was to evaluate her as a possible reining prospect. I wasn't completely surprised when I discovered that the mare was not at all what her owner said she was. This mare was a problem with hooves. She was a pretty problem, which is what got her a home in the first place. Beautiful faces don't always come with beautiful minds.

My customer didn't understand her mare's issues. Not even when the seller told her she couldn't buy the horse unless she took her to a trainer. In other words, the mare was dangerous. I messed with the mare on the ground then rode her a bit to check her buttons and figure out where training was needed and where obedience was needed. The initial results were not encouraging. After a couple of rides, I asked my customer a few more detailed questions.

I learned that Lizzie was sired by an idiot stallion and out of a mare used as a broodmare because she was too dangerous to ride. Hopefully you'll immediately grasp the problem. If not, let me spell it out. You get what you breed. If you breed an idiot, you'll likely get an idiot. It is a truism that the one characteristic you DO NOT want reproduced in a foal is the one you'll most certainly get. There are exceptions, but why accept such long odds with so many great horses already on the ground?

Knowing more about what I had to deal with, I worked my plan with the inconsistent, unreliable, unruly mare. Lizzie had issues with her ears, so I taught her to be led by an ear. Turning left was a problem, so we learned a left posture and moved every which way possible until she could stay upright and balanced going to the left. She got tight and pissy at any gait faster than a jog. By this I mean she would kick out at my legs or reach around to bite my feet. Just when I thought she was making progress she'd find a new way to express herself. This went on for about sixty days. By then I could do all the basics with her with apparent softness and correct form. But did I trust pretty Lizzie? No.

My customer was suitably impressed with our accomplishments and began to think her original assessment of the mare was brilliant. I tried to tell her otherwise, but see she didn't quite buy my opinion. Her horse did well when she watched me ride her. Indeed, my customer could now ride the mare and do more than she believed possible in such a short time. However, the mare wasn't personally invested in the program yet. I taught her that proper responses always included softness, relaxation, and obedience. She was giving me lip service and was coming along, but I wouldn't bet a nickel bet on her if push came to shove.

Just as I was about to hang it up on Lizzie she had a breakthrough. I trusted her enough to consider putting one of my good saddles on her. Until I know a horse won't rub me or the saddle into the ground or a pipe fence it wears a two-year-old saddle. I set aside a few well-worn saddles to use on young horses. They can roll in them, chew, rub, and I don't care a whit. This day I put one of my favorite saddles on the mare. Silly me. Lizzie stood tied in the grooming rack as she was every day. She'd been groomed, vacuumed, and tacked up there at least five days a week for two months. We'd worked through the issues of sheets, blankets, ears, and the rest of her many problems.

For no apparent reason (and usually there is an apparent reason) Lizzie sat back, broke her lead rope, and tumbled over backwards onto the concrete floor. The grooming areas were covered with rubber mats, but the mare went far enough backwards to get off them. Was Lizzie injured? Nope. Was my saddle? Yup.

What's the point of this story? When the mare stood up she hurried over, begging me to save her sorry behind. I said, "Well, sure." After that, she was obedient, putting everything she had into her lessons. Lizzie decided that I was the best thing on earth, even better than her alfalfa. She was dominated into obedience and relationship. Like the stallion my friend had, we reaped the benefit of what a horse associated with us even though we really weren't responsible for the circumstances.

I don't know what happened to the stallion my friend had in training, but I can tell you how Lizzie ended up. She was a broke horse after that but didn't transfer her devotion to me to other riders. She would obey, but she wouldn't offer herself up in relationship except to me. The last I heard she was riding fine but would not make a personal commitment to her new trainer or owner.

Sometimes it happens that way. I feel bad making a promise to the horse that I break by sending it home. That's the main reason I retired from breeding and training. Even if my body could stand the work, I don't feel right asking horses to trust me with relationship when I know I won't be keeping them. I can't do it anymore, not even in the short term.

Bob Gets a Home

When the property on our north border sold, the sorrel gelding living there, whom we called Bob, had to move. Except for our horses, my husband, and me, no one had noticed Bob for years. The Lord kept him fed and watered with grass and a tank in the large pasture where he lived. Bob had come to know us a bit and seemed a decent fellow.

One Sunday afternoon we noticed someone in the pasture trying unsuccessfully to catch Bob. We learned that the property sale was closing in the morning and Bob had to be removed immediately. Of course, the harder you try to catch a horse, the less likely you are to get the job done. Bob was a typical horse, and little progress was being made.

As evening neared, I asked the man standing there with a rope around Bob's neck if he needed help. He couldn't lead Bob and he needed to get him up to the house and into a waiting trailer. Bob's new owners were ready to take him home. We were thrilled Bob was going to have a home, so I went to the barn to get my serious training gear - a rope halter and long lead rope.

I'd never stood next to Bob without a double fence between us. He was taller than I thought and, upon closer inspection, appeared to be more likely a thoroughbred than the quarter horse I assumed he was. After the proper introductory body language, I haltered Bob. The house and waiting trailer were about two hundred feet away. For a while we danced. I suggested turns and let him find his way without putting any tension on the lead rope. We turned right and left; he yielded his hindquarters. I petted Bob and asked for his trust. He gave it in spades. In no time, we arrived at the yard where I could see the trailer waiting for Bob. Oh, dear.

Bob's new owners did the best they could on such short notice to come up with a way to transport him to his new home about five miles away. When you turn off our road, the farm to market road between where we were and where they were going is regularly traveled by semis used in the gas and oil drilling industry. Normal speeds often exceed sixty miles per hour.

Bob and I found a small tractor hitched to a flatbed trailer. The trailer had temporary (and wiggly) sides made from thin sheets of plywood. There was no back. I assumed the plan was to tie Bob to the front (front what, I had no idea) and drag the trailer home at maybe five miles per hour. After assessing the situation, I had no doubt about one thing: I would never violate the trust Bob had placed in me by asking him to get onto that flatbed. No debate, I told Bob's new owners exactly that. Bob had exhibited great character and wonderful obedience in a short time. I wouldn't betray him by setting him up to be injured or worse.

WE decided on a plan as the sun neared the western horizon. My husband went home, hooked up our ramped horse trailer and drove it over to. We would take Bob to his new home. It was the least we could do. This wasn't my first choice. Taking Bob to his new home meant I'd know where he was going and what his circumstances would be. Sometimes we're blessed by not knowing.

The next step was getting Bob into our trailer. Our trailer is the usual slant load with rear tack compartment, so the horse entry door is about thirty-six inches wide. Not very inviting for a horse that hasn't even seen shelter for who knows how many years. Yet Bob learned quickly. When needed, I insisted that he make the appropriate movements using the end of my lead rope on his hip. I trained him to move forward, to turn, and to be obedient. Loading a horse in a trailer to me is trailer training. I don't want to just get the horse loaded; I want to build foundation for the next time the horse needs to load and the time after that.

Bob's new owners watched and listened attentively as I gave a mini-clinic in the psychology of horses and how one should relate to them. They asked lots of great questions, which showed me they were committed to providing a good and appropriate home for Bob.

As darkness fell, Bob completed his lessons and loaded quietly into the trailer for about the sixth time (I always like to start with six times.) Off we went. Bob unloaded in a gravel parking area across the street from his new home. He led obediently and without any obvious concern to his new grass paddock. Bob was home. Bob had a family. Bob would be fine. I left my business card with Bob's new family in case they got into trouble.

We see Bob every now and then as we drive through the back streets of our tiny town. His owners erected a new roomy shelter within days of his arrival. Bob is fat, shiny, and loved. My husband and I regularly prayed for a home for Bob. Our prayers were answered, and we are grateful.

Balancing Authority and Humility

One of the greatest challenges many horse owners encounter is getting their horse in and out of a trailer. Without proper leadership and trust, horses may see trailers as either a threat. Others consider trailer loading a competition to see who can out-stubborn the other. Owners without the skills to properly train their horse often resort to brutish methods when trailer loading battles frustrate them. Jeremiah (10:21) gave the cause of Israel's calamity as "the shepherds have become senseless (brutish)"; that is, they acted on their own and did not seek God's wisdom and guidance. They did not deal wisely with their fellows. The Israelites devolved into beastly behavior, choosing to dominate whether necessary or not. Brutality isn't part of God's nature. Trainers who rely on dominating horses lack sufficient wisdom. Their toolbox quickly empties until nothing remains but brutality.

Other trainers may be efficient but have no joy in their work. Many horse trainers of the 1970s and 1980s didn't even like horses. They grew up in horse families where training horses was their only means to pay mortgages and feed families. Owning no affection for the horse, these trainer-horse relationships fell victim to dominance and submission. In other cases, trainers may experience early success with one special horse and try unsuccessfully for years afterwards to replicate it. With each failure, the trainer got more frustrated. Horses usually pay the price of human frustration.

Even trainers who consider themselves horse whisperers can resort to brutish methods out of ignorance. I witness it on a regular basis and was probably guilty of it somewhere along the line. The trainer thinks he's being relational, acting as a worthy leader - being moral - yet he deceives himself. No human leader or horse trainer ever lived who didn't need someone else to provide perspective or guidance on occasion. Proper authority requires balance with equal parts of humility. When we don't get the result we want, we must search out wisdom and direction from another source.

For whoever exalts himself will be humbled and he who humbles himself will be exalted. ~ Luke 14:11

Without understanding how to be rightly related to God it's difficult, if not impossible, to create a right relationship (non-brutish) with a horse. If you're stubborn before the Lord, you will wrongly transfer that motivation to your horse. You stiffen your neck in rebellion, then assume your horse's neck is stiff for the same reason. Couldn't stubbornness be the reason for ole' Sorrel's stiff neck? Possibly, but not probably. It's human nature, not the horse's nature, to believe everyone and everything else works the same way we do. If I'm greedy I believe everyone else is greedy. If I'm trusting, I assume everyone else is trusting. If I cheat, I'll take it for granted that everyone else cheats. If I'm loving I look for love in others.

Doing Battle

How do we build leadership and training skills? What's most important? Humility and authority must be balanced before you can understand and replicate right relationship. When balanced, we won't resort to dominance unless it's truly what the situation requires. Dominance is only properly used when a horse or human challenges us and there is no other way to resolve the matter.

Please understand, resorting to dominance is choosing to enter battle. Victory belongs to whoever is dominant when the battle ends. Is it ever appropriate to dominate a foal? As mentioned earlier, sometimes it is. The weapons of battle with a baby are radically different than those used with a mature horse, but the concepts and strategies are the same. Is it ever appropriate to dominate a human infant? Never.

Dominance is only correct when war is the only option remaining on the table. War must not be unilateral. Initiating a battle is brutishness if the opposition doesn't intend (or has no capacity) to wage war right back at you.

The only exception to a balanced equation of humility and authority is God Himself. There is no higher authority than the Father. Jesus Christ is the perfect example of perfectly balanced humility and authority. The New Testament is the best textbook for leaders as well as horse trainers. The United States is experiencing a crisis of leadership for this very reason; those in authority have misplaced any humility they may once have owned. As in

Jeremiah's day, our leaders have become brutish, drawing only from their own understanding. When results (inevitably) fail to meet expectations, our government resorts to using dominating and restrictive methods to lead the people they profess to serve.

I'm pleased to clean stalls and the 101 other interesting tasks required of horse homemakers, most of which are guaranteed to ruin a fresh manicure. How many of our political leaders would be content to wash the feet of their constituents? Would they even consent to wash each other's feet? Exactly how do they define public servant?

One cannot wield authority properly without being properly under authority. Trainers can't be good leaders unless properly led themselves. In day-to-day horse training operations, individuals hoping to learn the head trainer's leadership and relational skills aspire to be apprentices. They learn to be correctly authoritative with a horse while under the authority of the head trainer. I understand how to be a good trainer and establish right relationships with my grays by reversing roles, using my relationship to God as the illustration that furthers my understanding. You all know that "absolute power corrupts absolutely." Why? Because absolute authority, by definition, is not balanced by any humility whatsoever.

At the Last Supper, against Peter's protestations, Jesus performed a most humble task and said,

If I then, your Lord and Teacher, have washed your feet, you also ought to wash one another's feet. For I have given you an example, that you should do as I have done to you. ~ John 13:14-15

As Christ was instructed, so He instructed the disciples. Once you grasp what it means to be absolutely without power or excuse in front of a sovereign and almighty God, you may begin to develop wisdom that serves both you and your horse well.

HABIT OR OBEDIENCE

In everything that (Hezekiah) undertook in the service of God's temple and in obedience to the law and commands, he sought his God and worked wholeheartedly. And so he prospered. ~ 2 Chronicles 31:21

Moral excellence comes about as a result of habit. We become just by doing just acts, temperate by doing temperate acts, brave by doing brave acts. ~ Aristotle

Bo and Copper partnered with us at a Texas Smokin' Guns mounted shooting practice match. We participate in Cowboy Mounted Shooting Association (CMSA) events, a unique sport combining fast riding, period western costume, and shooting balloon targets with single-action .45 caliber revolvers. It's fun. The CMSA has competition levels suitable for every rider regardless of skill level and value of the horse. Unlike breed association competitions, horses in CMSA events need only be sound and have a name. Okay, they don't really have to have a name, but the announcer must call them something.

Bo and Copper have only gone to shoots every few months for the past year and aren't seasoned shooting horses. After years on the horse show circuit, Baber and I don't enjoy traveling long distances and we shoot for fun. Bo is coming along well. My priority is building foundation and confidence. I want Bo and Swizzle to do whatever I ask with confidence and, when necessary, with boldness. So far, Bo and I haven't had any significant setbacks to interfere with this goal.

Baber and Copper, however, have had several bumps along the road. They're both in remedial mode, going back to the beginning to rebuild their confidence. Relearning is never as easy as avoiding problems, but Baber and Copper making good progress. At yesterday's practice, Baber rode Copper with acceptable, though limited, results. I rode Bo.

When not running the pattern ourselves, Bo and I worked balloon duty. Each run uses ten balloons; five each of two different colors. After each run the balloons are replaced and ready for the next competitor. All that's left is a balloon remnant on a wooden dowel used to hold it on the end of a PVC pole. Bo and I love to pick up sticks. We practice maneuvering with minimal cues and Bo gets used to being on course in a completely relaxed manner.

Bo was good until his unshod feet got a bit tender the parking lot stones. Once getting protective boots he was happy again. Bo is never owly. It took me a few minutes to realize that his mild ear pinning and head-tossing meant he was uncomfortable. The boots made him *able* to perform comfortably and he was himself again.

You're responsible for figuring out why your horse behaves out of character, then doing whatever is necessary to resolve the problem. Physical discomfort is the first possibility to investigate. There's more accountability to resolve the smallest objections with obedient and stable horses. Horses with great temperaments seldom create big problems until they're in severe pain.

Copper did well considering the last couple of times he and Baber entered the shooting arena were difficult or downright disastrous. Copper now tests a rider for leadership since experience has proved it's not always present. All trainers make mistakes and inexperienced riders make more in stressful environments.

Copper and I picked up sticks until he would guide and rate mostly with balance and "leg." I decided to test his obedience by riding a stage (riding a full course, shooting the balloon targets at speed). With his history, I was only 90-percent sure Copper would perform confidently. Knowing there was a 10-percent chance he'd get into a bind, Plan B was ready if he acted out, making the remedy more of a problem than a solution.

Copper was perfect! He was delightfully obedient and I passed his leadership test. With this happy result, I pulled his saddle, curried his coat, and retired him for the day.

After an excellent final stage, Bo and I stopped at the water barrel before going back to the trailer. Bo hasn't figured out how to drink efficiently with a bit in his mouth. He sounds like a kid trying to get the last drop out of a plastic cup with a straw; kinda like a splurty vacuum. It was a warm day and Bo needed sufficient water so I rode him back to the trailer to remove his bridle and put on a halter. While we were still at the water barrel, I considered dropping the bridle and leading him back to the trailer with just a rein around his neck. It would probably have worked just fine, but we were next to a very busy highway and I wasn't going to chance it.

At the trailer I patted him, hugged his head, took off his bridle, and put on a rope halter. I was just about to loosen his girth when I decided my knees had taken all they could handle for the day.

It was time for a pop quiz to test Bo's level of obedience. The quiz, of course, was really to test my leadership. I remounted with the lead rope in my left hand. I'd never ridden Bo with a single rein away from home.

169

Off to the water barrel we rode. Bo responded exactly as he would with a bridle and reins. Shooters were still competing as Bo took a deep, long drink. I sat on him, enjoying a quiet moment together - cherished companionship amid the bustle, traffic, and gunfire.

Maybe it was time to give Bo a more difficult quiz. He aced the pop quiz of riding about with little more than just my legs for direction. Was it reasonable to expect Bo to be obedient if we went back into the arena to retrieve sticks with no bridle; just a halter and lead rope? So far, all my cues of balance and leg worked perfectly. Bo was as honest and responsive as he had been with a bridle.

Even if Bo wasn't ready guide in the arena without a bridle, guns blazing, and horses racing around at breakneck speeds -- I did trust him to be reasonable and listen to me. After due consideration, I determined that no one's safety would be jeopardized if we left bridle behind.

I'd already tested "whoa" without using any rein cues and was confident that whatever other issues might arise, Bo would stop if I asked. Into the arena we went, barely squeezing through the aisle nearly blocked by three riders watching the competition and chatting.

I sent Bo down the line of cones and poles to pick up sticks at a rapid trot, turning easily as we negotiated the course. Perfect! We loped back to the balloon staging area to turn in the sticks. Side-passing to the waiting bucket, I dropped the sticks over the fence and returned to the end of the arena to wait for the next shooter to finish. No one even noticed Bo wasn't wearing a bridle, not even my husband. I love this horse!

After the next shooter screamed across the finish line toward us, Bo and I headed out again to pick up the sticks, taking a different path through the cones than the last time. I guided him briskly toward the farthest cone, the one nearest the spot where Bo and I had spent most of our day waiting during runs.

Habit of task kicked in. I tried to steer Bo away from our usual resting place where he thought we were heading. He didn't turn away from my instruction—he didn't turn at all. Instead of making a 90 degree turn to the right as my balance and leg requested, Bo continued straight toward the arena fence, about thirty feet ahead. Not far to the left was our usual spot. Bo had returned to that place all day long. I knew he thought we should be going there, which required a left turn. But my request was to turn right, but I didn't have a right rein. Using the fence to my advantage, I pushed the lead rope up his neck a bit (usually I neck rein at the shoulder) to communicate a boundary and exaggerated my left leg position. I simply held those cues until Bo figured it out. Habit of task had created the confusion; habit of obedience resolved it.

Quit While You're Ahead

We loped off again in good order. A glimmer of doubt dawned in my mind. Bo might realize there were options other than obedience after this exercise, so I did what any good leader would do in the circumstances. We quit on a high note. I rode Bo back to the trailer. Bo finished the quiz with 100-percent correct responses. I dismounted, pulled his saddle, and gave him a good rub down and a carrot.

What did I learn? First, I remembered to check my motivation before beginning the exercise. Was I just trying to show off? Maybe just a little. I'm only human. Bo was a star. Copper also passed his own test of obedience with flying colors. We have more work to do and goals to achieve, but this was a very good day.

172

AMAZING GRAYS, AMAZING GRACE

THE 153 FISH PRINCIPLE

The disciples "got into the boat, and that night they caught nothing."

And He said to them, "Cast the net on the right side of the boat, and you will find some." So they cast, and now they were not able to draw it in because of the multitude of fish.

Jesus said to them, "Bring some of the fish which you have just caught." Simon Peter went up and dragged the net to land, full of large fish, one hundred and fifty-three; and although there were so many, the net was not broken. ~ John 21:3, 6, 10, 11

When I work through a weighty lesson with Bo or Swizzle, the Lord takes the opportunity to give me a corresponding lesson. Whenever my ego balloon starts getting a little over inflated I can count on the Lord (or a horse) to let a whole lot of air out. And that's a good thing, 'cause too much air can burst a balloon. On this morning, the Lord showed me how the test of obedience applied to me. God is so amazing. Each time this "coincidence" of parallel training occurs, I'm less surprised. I am also, increasingly grateful that He loves me enough to continue my training day after day.

Much has been written about the mystery of the 153 fish caught by the disciples in the twenty-first chapter of John.

Because the content is so precise, "153 fish" and "the net did not break", biblical scholars surmise that there must be a great message to Christians hidden in these gospel verses. Most speculation involves the number itself, 153.

Commentary on these verses include a host of machinations, algebraic formulae, and intricate calculations suggesting how the number 153 may be significant. The simplest explanation is that the number 153 represented the total number of fish species in the sea, perhaps a metaphor for all the peoples on earth. Since there are more than 153 species, that theory was proven to be false.

Other equations deal with the number of days Jesus lived on earth: 12,240 (153 x 80). Others note that Jesus' ministry lasted 918 days, or 153 multiplied by 6. There are many sources who believe the number 153 to be significant as it relates to the number of generations from Adam to Christ and beyond, 77 plus 76. This equation always includes a footnote, as the numbers don't quite work out without some qualification.

May I suggest another explanation of the story? As a simple soul, the creative ways others use to prove the number 153 significant are interesting but not particularly meaningful to me. How do mathematical exercises assist us in our daily walk with Jesus Christ? The story of the 153 fish begins, "In this way Jesus showed Himself" (NKJV) to the disciples a third and final time before returning to sit at God's right hand.

In this way, what I call the "153 Fish Principle" is the application of the gospel's message in one short story. Jesus gave the disciples and, indeed, all Christians, one final, perfect illustration of how we are to live in right relationship to Him. In these verses, we find seven disciples fishing—men who specifically called and chosen to build the church of Christ and who shared His ministry. They had already been selected to receive the Holy Spirit and carry on the ministry of Jesus Christ.

Remember, they were experienced fishermen. They weren't weekend anglers. The seven disciples set out that night to fish by their own choice, doing what they knew how to do. The Holy Spirit sent them out on their ultimate missions later. These disciples, these expert fishermen, spent that dark, barren night working, letting the net down again and again, only to haul it back empty. Imagine their frustration, doing what they knew how to do but experiencing complete and exhausting failure.

Jesus instructed His disciples one final time. He told them what to do, "Cast your net." He told them where to cast it, "on the right side of the boat"; and He told them when to act—to act now. The disciple's expertise at fishing yielded nothing. The fact that they had physically walked with Jesus Christ did not produce success. The key to success was obedience to His direction, resulting in the incredible, abundant fruit of 153 large fish.

Obedience to Jesus Christ produced the miraculous catch, not the election of the disciples and not their specific knowledge of fishing. What was Jesus telling these men this one last time before sending them off on to ministry and likely martyrdom? Jesus showed them (and us) that a right relationship with Him produces obedience. Success is only achieved by obedience.

Not long before I realized I was writing this book I returned to a business consulting practice that had been mostly dormant during my years in the horse industry. After six months in near retirement the Lord gave me a new assignment. He was specific and thorough. I was surprised and pleased to discover I was still capable and relevant. It was clear that I now worked for God; at His direction and at His pace. He cleared the road when needed and opened doors before me. I basked in the luxury of working His plan at His direction. As time progressed, I tried to sit in the manager's chair, reviewing marketing and promotion options to build my practice. I knew how to do it. I'd done it before.

I began to worry (well, I didn't worry, but considered) what my next moves should be for my consulting practice. Then the answer came. It wasn't a new message but confirmation of what I already knew. Confirmation came with my experience with Bo at the Texas Smokin' Guns practice where he defaulted to the habit of task until my gentle correction brought him back into obedience. The message was to avoid reverting to the habit of task, doing what I knew how to do. I was gently but firmly informed that I was to remain obedient and wait for instruction from the Boss.

My work is no longer mine to direct. I'm in a new phase of my relationship with the Lord. The habit of task must be replaced with the habit of obedience. It's not a quick work and I know there will still be tests I won't ace. In the meantime, Bo and Swizzle are wonderful gifts of delightful relationship, and they serve as illustrations of lessons meant specifically for me.

The story of Jesus and His disciple fishermen is on point for the lesson I learned today and hope to remember tomorrow when temptation to revert to task arises again. Peter and the disciples fished all through the long night without success. They caught absolutely nothing.

The first time Jesus (the Spirit) told me to cast my net, it delivered an unlikely first assignment, years away and far removed geographically from my prior work. I was given a huge project and allowed to complete it well.

The next specific task was this book, *Amazing Grays, Amazing Grace*. I expected to return to consulting and speaking. It never thought I'd be writing, especially on a non-business subject.

The "153 Fish Principle" is simple: do *what* Jesus instructs, *where* He instructs, and *when* He instructs. Rest all on Him, not on your own abilities and talents. Apart from Jesus Christ, is only exhausting failure. Leave behind the long, dark, cold, unproductive nights of self-direction. Obedience will yield success.

My conclusion? I'll cast my net where and when He tells me. That's my job. I'm confident that in His time I'll receive instruction for new catches. My obedience all I bring. In return, I am blessed by relationship with Him.

TEST OF LEADERSHIP

Not that I have already attained, or am already perfected; but I press on, that I may lay hold of that for which Jesus Christ has also laid hold of me. ~ Philippians 3:12

How we spend our days is, of course, how we spend our lives. ~ Annie Dillard

When comparing the habit of task and the habit of obedience we discover two major differences: one builds foundation for future learning, the other does not; and one builds relationship, the other does not. Someone once said that bad habits are like a soft chair—easy to get in to but hard to get out of.

One early spring weekend we hauled to Cleburne, Texas, for another practice shoot. It was a new arena for us. Copper and I warmed up first. As the trainer for both Baber and Copper, I'm responsible for their safety and building confidence rather than patterns of inconsistency.

Copper offered a lesson about tests of leadership from a horse's perspective. Baber and Copper experienced a noteworthy wreck when first competing in mounted shooting. At the, Copper was more confident than Bo, and it seemed that he and Baber would be the shooting stars of the family.

However, the foundation they had to work with was not strong enough. Events compounded until the crisis Copper found in Baber's leadership resulted in mutually bad experiences.

Bo and I have slowly and steadily built our confidence without any setbacks or difficult places. I'm careful to only ask what Bo is ready to give, and I'm a fanatic for getting correct before asking for fast. Everything proceeds in an orderly fashion even if it seems like we spent a year in kindergarten. In a way, we did. Bo was barely broke when we started going to shooting matches. Sometimes taking things slowly is the fastest route to ultimate success. As a result, Bo went from kindergarten to middle school in a few months, then to completely skipped high school to address college-level lessons.

Because of Copper's bad experiences, he went to remedial classes to work through the issues created by the smash ups. I wasn't personally involved in the wrecks, but ultimately, they were my responsibility. I didn't supervise Copper's education with Baber closely enough. It was my failure that left Baber and Copper with more confidence in having a bad outcome than a good one. At least I know how to fix the mess I made. It only took one or two events to seriously damage Copper and Baber's relationship—at least at shooting matches.

The good news is they're doing better. Now it's imperative that I structure every ride to build Copper's obedience and confidence in our leadership.

Copper's wonderful nature taught me a lesson about leadership that day in Cleburne. I rode him around the unfamiliar arena, looking for any places where he might tighten up or exhibit fear. I was working to create the habit of task in this new environment and the habit of obedience in our relationship. I promise horses I train that I will never ask them to do anything that will hurt them. They are free to obey without fear. Since Copper knew that my leadership record with him was less than perfect, he decided to put it to the test. What a smart horse.

Copper worked nicely in the arena, loose and relaxed. He accepted pressure and offered correct responses. I considered limiting his warm up to walking, trotting, turning, and stopping properly and lightly. If I didn't include loping as part of today's habit, Copper would be less likely to misinterpret a cue from Baber as a request to lope.

Baber is uncertain when riding faster than at a trot. Part of Copper's remedial training is creating new physical habits and frame at the lope. He need to create new muscle memory. Copper left lead needs work. We need to practice until the correct form is his default form.

The Test

Sometimes the plan to exclude an exercise is a good one; sometimes it's not. There's no one right, absolute answer to any question regarding horses. It's important to know what motivates your decision. Am I making the situation safer or avoiding one of those troublesome doors. Was I afraid Copper would be disobedient if I asked him to lope, requiring me to fix it at an inopportune time? I decided to skip the lope and rode back to the trailer so Baber could ride.

Copper and I left the arena through a different gate from the one we had entered. Tucked in behind a rail fence and paneled gates was a set of wheels on axles. Each axle had an old wheel on one end, the other resting in the dirt. They reminded me of the tinker toys I played with as a child. Fences formed a twenty-foot wide alleyway from the gate exiting the arena to another about sixty feet away. The alley fences formed one side of pipe pens built on either side of the alley.

Copper saw the wheels hiding behind the fence, sucked his body backwards like the tide going out, and gave every indication he was prepared to flee. I firmly, but gently, kept him facing those fearsome monster wheels for about five seconds. I knew they wouldn't move or make any sound, so there was no valid reason for Copper to be concerned about those hunks of iron. His behavior surprised me, since Copper isn't usually a spooky horse. Go figure.

I asked him to take one step toward the wheels, then stop. In similar situations, don't wait for your horse to decide to stop - tell him when to stop. Remember, whoever controls the feet wins. Always keep your horse in a place of obedience.

If you think your horse may refuse to go forward, ask him to back up. Then ask for one or two steps forward. Stop. Relax. Pretend you haven't a care in the world. Continue forward a step or two at a time. Stop. Relax. Remember, your horse must be moving when you say whoa. If this doesn't work or your horse sulls up and won't go forward, steer into a different angle and try again.

Copper stepped forward. I asked him to stop. After another second or two, I asked him to walk by the wheels. There was limited area in the alley to work with, and Copper put as much distance between himself and those wheels as the fence allowed. I didn't allow him to cheat his form; I maintained correct movement and position, requiring Copper to go where I asked. I walked him by the wheels a few more times until he looked at them and became soft and obedient.

We left the arena. Baber got on Copper and I got on Bo for the first time that day. I warned Baber about Copper's reaction to the wheels and gave him instructions on what to do if Copper reacted to the wheels. Not surprisingly, when they rode by the wheels, Copper didn't appear to remember that they existed, much less that he acted like they might eat him five minutes earlier. Copper was so cool butter wouldn't have melted.

The Lord showed me that the wheel exercise was a test of my leadership. Horses are smart. We just need to take the time to understand them. Copper wasn't going to wait until something of real concern popped before finding out if my leadership was up to his requirements. Copper wanted to know at the get-go if he could trust me.

God's Word tells us that if we cannot be trusted with small things, how can we be trusted with important things? As Jesus said in John 3:12, "If I have told you earthly things and you do not believe, how will you believe if I tell you heavenly things?"

This is exactly the test Copper gave me. He wanted to know if he could believe me in a simple matter; the wheels. If I failed that small test, there was no way he would follow my lead in a serious matter, like shooting guns.

After Copper and Baber had hung out in the arena for a while, I noticed that Copper was responding increasing less precisely to what Baber asked him to do. Baber was getting less confident and so was Copper. It was time for Copper and me to ride again. Baber took Bo back to the trailer and I got back on Copper.

I decided to up the ante. It was time to lope. I asked Copper to pick up a nice, easy lope. He gave me a half-hearted crow hop before taking the lead I'd requested. Wrong answer. I pulled him around quickly, and while he was curled like a cat, I used my spur to send his hip in a circle around his front end. Once he gave completely to the pressure, I lined him out straight again and without hesitation asked for a right lead again.

This time Copper was as sweet and light as he could be. We toured around at an easy lope for a few moments before I

183

asked him to pick up his left lead, the one that's more difficult for him. Copper was obedient. I patted his rump and scratched his neck as we loped around the pen. I decided to run a full shooting pattern on him, gunfire and all. The habit of obedience won the day. Copper did precisely as I asked and was a happy camper from the time we crossed the timer line at the beginning of the run to crossing again at the end. Copper tried me, I passed his test, and his confidence in my direction grew. What a glorious day.

Another Amazing Gray

When building a habit of obedience, do we teach horses to always ask for permission before reacting to a stimulus? Absolutely not. I want the benefit that a horse's superior vision and hearing bring to the relationship. Good trainers want to preserve their horse's freedom and personality. When horses spook or refuse to obey, there's only a split second to determine if there's a valid reason for the horse's negative response. The situation must be handled appropriately.

Years ago, a gray quarter horse gelding came in for training. My customer liked the horse, but she was frustrated when he quit loping and he stopped on his front end rather than from behind, as is correct and most comfortable. My job was to tune-up him up so he could be sold.

This gelding was a stout, good-looking fellow and sure seemed to be kind. My habit was to do each horse's daily lesson in the arena and then ride out into the desert to cool off and see how well the horse handled trail riding. This routine revealed hidden issues with traffic, birds, animals, terrain, or unexpected situations. When I represented a horse, I wanted to know as much as possible so I could fix any problem that surfaced, or at least accurately relate strengths and weaknesses to prospective buyers.

One day this good gray gelding and I were out in the desert when he abruptly stopped. No prancing, no

184

nervousness, and no apparent reason for coming to a dead stop. I asked him to move forward. He very politely refused. *What in the world is wrong with this horse?* I was puzzled. I asked him to move forward again. Again, he politely refused and continued to calmly stand rooted to that spot.

Then I saw it: a rattlesnake coiled under a creosote bush five feet in front of us. What a great horse. He refused to obey my request to move forward because he had more information about the situation than I did. He was perfectly polite in his refusal. I give the benefit of my doubt to the horse. Although my requests for him to move forward were firm, they never escalated past firm. That marvelous gray didn't escalate his refusal, remaining polite, so I returned the favor. If this gelding had been taught to always yield to his rider without question, we may have found ourselves in a bad situation. That gray took care of me. I was grateful. I acknowledged the snake, petted the gelding's neck, and guided him in a wide berth around the rattler.

I schooled this good gray gelding's lope and stop. It really wasn't that difficult a task. I asked my customer to come ride him and check my work. She was a good-sized lady without great hands or seat—in other words, she wasn't a well-schooled rider. As she rode the gray's issues began to resurface. She asked him to lope. He was immediately obedient but didn't lope for long. He just stopped. She tried again, so did he. Again, he stopped. Before she got on I'd demonstrated well he performed. He loped beautifully and stopped on a dime. He didn't quit when I rode him. Before she could get frustrated, I explained why that good gray gelding was quitting with her.

My customer wasn't petite or a well-schooled rider. When the good gray picked up a lope she began to lose her balance. Each successive stride put her closer to the point where she could have bounced out of the saddle completely. As soon as her situation became precarious, her horse would

LYNN BABER

stop and quietly stand, allowing her to get back in the middle of the saddle. That wonderful gray gelding was taking care of her as he had with me out in the desert. What a guy. If I could have, I'd have bought him on the spot. Even though he had to be uncomfortable with his rider's lack of skill, he still did whatever she asked until his greater experience and kindly concern for her prevailed and he stopped.

My customer deserves a lot credit for understanding and appreciating the situation. She didn't have a decent horse with a couple of issues; she had a great horse that could be counted on to take care of her in any situation. She had her very own amazing gray. I am pleased to report that he was no longer for sale at any price. My customer decided that riding lessons would be a good idea, bless her heart. I loved my customers, and I love happy endings.

I want obedience and patience from my horses. I also want them to be confident and free to teach me when necessary. Worthwhile relationships aren't one-sided. No one can be a great leader if no one is willing to follow. God requires obedience and commitment from us. Yet He leaves us free to exhibit the unique personalities He gave us. Unlike me, He knows where all the snakes are, but the essence of the lesson is the same.

Do you have the habit of task or of obedience? Do you yield from pain or through obedience? Are you wonderfully confident in your relationship with Jesus Christ? As you blissfully proceed along life's path, have you ever been stopped short without an obvious explanation? Perhaps there's a snake hiding in front of you. Be very careful before pushing ahead. Some obstacles teach us to overcome while others block the way, forcing us to redirect our feet.

Copper taught me to be a better leader and a better follower. That good gray gelding taught me that things are not always what they first appear to be, and sometimes the best plan is to listen rather than to direct.

186

OBEDIENCE AND BONDING

And this is love: that we walk in obedience to his commands. ~ 2
John 6 (NIV)

Obedience without faith is possible, but not faith without obedience.
~ Unknown

Building relationship is a progressive exercise. Attraction may
be instantaneous; but strong, meaningful relationships are
made in an orderly, predictable manner. Even the relationship
between a mother and her child follows an established path
of development. The initial attraction is physical as the baby
moves during pregnancy. At birth, strong hormones create a
powerful attraction and the bonding process continues.

Many research studies prove the link between hormones
and physical touch and the emotional cord that connects
mother and child throughout their lifetimes. Fathers are first
bound to their children by the relationship they share with
the mother. A separate relationship begins in its own
structured and predictable way when the father starts
physically caring for the child, committing time, energy, and
proximity to his offspring. Proximity is of utmost importance.
Absent fathers and mothers don't enjoy elementally strong
relationships with their children.

Anyone who has raised a child can testify to the need for a strong bond with his or her infant. If not for that great love, most two-year-olds would be shipped off to military preschool. Hormones initiate protective feelings; relationship supports and enhances them. Without relationships, the stress of caring for children could easily exceed the perceived benefit. We do it for love.

From the child's perspective, relationships with the mother starts with simple need. Nourishment, warmth, and protection are given by the mother and father. An infant's universe only extends to the humans who care for her. As the child grows and matures, her world enlarges. This expansion offers greater variety and opportunity for relationships with others besides the parents. Siblings become recognizable as separate humans. The child becomes aware of, then processes, her environment. Soon she is aware of people outside the family. Preferences begin to emerge as the child's personality forms and is expressed.

At this very early stage, the habit of obedience, or lack thereof, begins. It's never too early to provide children with structure and boundaries as they learn more about loving relationships. Structure and boundaries are vital parts of any strong, meaningful relationship. Structure, boundaries, and consistency are the pillars that support security, trust, and confidence.

Mares, Foals, and Me

In horses, the mare-foal relationship is like that of a human mother and child. The degree to which a mare understands who causes the movement in her belly during pregnancy is unknown, but God handles the matter with hormones. From conception through birth, hormones are busy, making the mare physically aware that she is pregnant. Hormones direct the body to pass the afterbirth, bond with the foal, and produce milk to nourish it. Like human mothers, most mares claim their foals soon after birth and defend them from all threats and predators.

The relationship building process begins as soon as the foal knows you're there. I've had the privilege of being present at more than a hundred foal births. I've literally caught more than one foal midway between the standing mare and the ground, trying to keep the umbilical cord intact long enough to complete the passive blood transfer. How effective and helpful I am to the foaling process depends on the strength and quality of my relationship with the mare.

One Thoroughbred maiden mare (having her first foal) and I enjoyed a particularly close relationship. When stage three labor began, Step had no idea what was happening. She whinnied and nickered for me to come hold her hoof. Step wanted me present to provide security and support. Together we welcomed a warm wet chestnut filly into the world. As frequently happens, we began our relationship while her hind feet were still inside the mare. Too soon? Certainly, not in this case.

There are as many opinions about how and when the human-foal bonding process should begin as there are for human babies. I believe only well-informed, experienced, emotionally-invested people should make the decisions. If you don't understand and love mothers, babies, and the entire birth process, your opinion may not be helpful. Book learning is fine, but some things require hands-on-down-in-the-wet-straw experience.

For years, I attended the birth of every foal. Expected foals were all valuable in an economic way in addition to their intrinsic worth as individuals. In most cases mares don't need help or want human interference. However, any complication during the foaling process is usually a matter of life and death.

I spent countless nights watching mares preparing to foal on closed-circuit TV, allowing me to decide when to show up at the stall. I discovered that most mares who know they're being observed get up and down during active labor more than those on camera. Left alone, mares often lay down in the spot they eventually give birth. Getting up and down is especially dangerous once the foal's front feet and head are delivered.

Over time I decided that well-adjusted mares should have plenty of private time with their new foals to let the bonding process proceed without interruption. After the first twenty-four hours, I began building relationship with the new baby. Even at this very early stage of life, structure, boundaries, and consistency are introduced.

Structure and boundaries were built on body language, space issues, and a quick resolution of any contest of wills. I used the method of communication foals are preprogrammed to understand. The foundation we lay in the first day or two of the foal's life remains in place as long as we have a relationship with it. Most good trainers today understand the techniques I use to construct a foundation I can build upon throughout the foal's life.

Even very young foals exhibit wrong behavior. There eventually comes a day when every spoiled or recalcitrant little brat needs to learn obedience. Horse lovers know that they need structure, safety, consistency, relationship (the herd), and accountability just like people. It's tragic when horse owners are ignorant of the facts. It is even more tragic when human parents ignore, or are ignorant of, the needs of their children.

There will always be a hard lesson in the future for foals that weren't taught structure and boundaries. They will be insecure and maybe even dangerous.

There will always be hard lessons in the future of human children who are not taught to respect boundaries and recognize when obedience is required. They're also more

190

likely to be insecure, unhappy, and potentially dangerous - if only to themselves. Children with self-destructive tendencies eventually become self-destructive adults if their paths are not changed.

Obedience is a habit. The habit of obedience is acquired over time with frequent, regular repetition of consistent experience until obedience is an automatic response. Practice, practice, practice.

Our relationship with God is built in the same way as the relationship of mother and child or mare and foal. It develops over time, requires structure and boundaries, consistency and proximity. Structure and boundaries are given to Christians in the Bible and through the work of the Holy Spirit. The first lesson we learn is obedience. If we do not, there will be correction and consequences. Once the habit of obedience is established, other lessons may be learned.

Children begin to learn words, reading, numbers, and how to interact with others outside the family. Horses move from simple obedience to more complex skills and maneuvers. Christians move to a deeper level of spiritual communion with the Lord, learning how to properly lead lives that glorify God. In every case, whether child, horse, or Christian, the habit of obedience must be regularly tested and maintained. Relationship only grows with the commitment of time, consideration, and proximity. Parents and horse trainers are responsible to be properly prepared before lessons begin. God is always prepared.

Relationship Triangles

The habit of obedience must be firmly in place before adding complications to the relationship of parent and child, trainer and horse, God and man.

Let's consider how adding another individual to the mix changes relationships. Bo is learning to be a pony horse. That means that I ride him leading another horse alongside. Bo is

191

required to willingly and softly go where I ask at whatever speed I ask. He should perform as if the second horse isn't even there. The horse being ponied is expected to stay on my right side (we'll add the left side later) with its head at my knee. Perfect positioning lets me to drop my right hand down to pet or scratch the horse being ponied on its forehead. Bo should guide from leg pressure and the one being led should remain in the right place without putting tension on the lead rope. The ponied horse is responsible to stay where it belongs without being reminded.

Bo is well on his way to being a great pony horse. He's proven that he can take a hard hit and remain steady if the ponied horse resists, sitting back with its full weight on the rope dallied to my saddle horn. Bo should walk, trot, or lope as requested, no matter what the other horse does. And, when asked, he's willing and able to move into the other horse, pushing its hip around when needed.

Once Bo moved from task-oriented work to relational work, the whole dynamic changed. Bo and Swizzle are part of a herd. They spend a lot of pasture time with Asti and Copper. Bo is higher than Swizzle in herd pecking order. Bo frequently pushes Swizzle around by putting pressure at her hip, driving her where he wants. This is Bo's normal relationship with Swizzle. They seek each other's company, but when push comes to shove, Bo is boss over Swizzle.

Bo and I have a well-established relationship. Where ponying is concerned, Bo displays a habit of obedience appropriate for his level of training. Swizzle knows how to be obedient as the ponied horse. Whether at a walk or trot, she keeps her forehead right at my hand or knee like she wasn't even haltered. Swizzle is confident in this arrangement; life makes sense to her. Bo, on the other hand, is now a little confused. I wonder if he thinks I am confused? Bo is steady as a rock when we pony Copper. He stays where I want, is straight as an arrow, guides and responds just as if Copper wasn't with us.

Bo is different when we pony Swizzle. He isn't exactly disobedient, but he tries to drift to the left, away from Swizzle, rather than tracking straight and easy. He keeps running into my left leg, and I must repeatedly cue him to get straight. He keeps a concerned right ear focused on Swizzle even though she's blissfully popping alongside without a care in the world. Why the difference? Why the different reaction from Bo? He's 100 percent obedient and solid when ponying good buddy Copper, but not sure he's completely with the program when ponying his little friend Swizzle. Bo needs to learn to obey even when he doesn't understand why he's being asked to do something that to him seems wrong.

Why would Bo think it wrong? Bo's habit of obedience is complicated by his relationship with Swizzle. From his perspective, this third wheel in our relationship equation isn't tracking correctly. Bo currently believes that the power position is off the hip of the other horse. When he moves Swizzle around the pasture, he is on her hip, gently pushing and driving her along. He's the top banana. As a pony horse, he leads with the other on his hip, as if it were driving or pushing him along. When we pony Swizzle, Bo thinks that his position relative to Swizzle is backwards and that she now holds the position of power. This reversal of status, in his mind anyway, taxes his commitment to obedience. He's doing well, but we have work to do. Bo must learn to obey no matter how bizarre the circumstances seem to him.

What I learned from Bo and Swizzle is to obey the Lord even when I don't understand the "why." It's hard to be obedient, especially when pride is involved. I marvel at just how obedient Bo is. Imagine you're forty years old with twenty years of experience as a registered nurse. You've been assigned to serve in a subordinate position to an eighteen-year-old in your church's annual flu-shot program. Not only is the kid not a health professional but you know he's lucky to get his shoes on the right foot each morning. How could you softly, happily, and obediently await his instruction? This is pretty much what Bo is thinking.

I know that Bo is in the power position. The horse off his hip isn't pushing him; Bo is leading. He just doesn't realize it yet. I see the big picture and so will Bo. he's just not quite there yet.

There's another lesson coming up for Bo and Swizzle. Right now Bo wants to correct Swizzle, to move her away from his hip. Swizzle doesn't expect Bo to react to her at all. She looks to me for direction. As Bo matures as a pony horse the day will come when he'll obey my direction, understanding where the horse being ponied belongs and that rules apply to them both. When he's ready, I'll delegate some responsibility for correcting the ponied horse to him. Bo could turn into a little tyrant if allowed to correct Swizzle now. The criteria he'd use for correction would be his own, not mine. That wouldn't be fair to Bo and grossly unfair to Swizzle.

Whether human or horse, young or old, individuals can turn into bullies when given premature authority. Tyrants are created when they get authority before having learned humility; when they rule subordinates from selfish, ego-driven motives.

A Higher Plan

My plans for Bo are well laid out. Each lesson leads to the next. Bo only sees today's lesson. He doesn't know that one day he'll carry me while I work another horse as if I were on the ground. He'll be my partner as we train other horses. My knees are almost shot. Bo has four good legs and will be a service horse as well as a working pony. I know he'll become the horse I intend him to be. I also haven't told him that he's going to learn to bow so I can get on without a mounting block. He'll do that too. He just can't see it yet.

All my plans for Bo depend on his habit of obedience and my ability to communicate each small step in a way he can process. Bo will learn to accept and do what I ask, even if he doesn't understand why I'm asking.

Plans for children begin this way. All God's plans for us begin this way. He has the plan all worked out, even though we can't see the future as He does. We don't know what the next step will be as we grow into who God plans for us to be. Success begins with our habit of obedience, even if we think the current lesson makes no sense.

Bo and Swizzle trust me enough to obey, and I'm only a simple person. How silly it is to think God doesn't know what He's doing. All we need do is calmly, quietly, and happily obey.

LEADING GROUPS

The sheep hear his voice; and he calls his own sheep by name and leads them out. ~ John 10:3

The best learning I had came from teaching. ~ Corrie Ten Boom

In the previous chapter, we learned that relationships are tested when an outsider is added to the equation. As obedient as Bo is, ponying Swizzle created a relationship triangle. The strength and parameters of my relationship with Bo were tested and found in need of reinforcement.

In my opinion, there are two basic ways to lead groups: a military style and a relational style. In the military style, all group members are trained the same. There are negative consequences for everyone when the leader's rules are broken. No allowance is given to individual differences whether physical, mental, aptitude, or preferential. All are judged the same.

The relational style of leading groups is like training horses. One illustration is the multi-horse acts of *Cavalia*, a multimedia stage presentation showcasing the bond between humans and horses. Each horse must be trained separately until it is so focused on the leader that it will remain obedient when another horse is added. Each successive horse is also trained individually. Relationship with each horse is tested when they are put together to perform. Corrections must be made individually.

The horses aren't really a team; they perform independently but in unison. Each horse must be in a right relationship with the trainer before being added to the act. If a horse needs additional work, it is separated and weak places strengthened before joining up with the others again.

Horses working in unison but trained in a relational style, never truly work as a team unless they experience the unifying experience of a military style of reward or consequence. It's possible to make great horse teams. Horses learn incrementally how to hold their position in a multi-horse hitch. Teams learn to pull together, discovering how they can minimize the load when they combine their efforts in synergistic rhythm. The yoke is equally shared.

Team spirit or connection is made when the members of the team are treated as parts of a whole, and not as individuals. What any member experiences, all members experience. There may be exceptions for gross violations of the rules, but the exception is well understood by others, and there is also a lesson for them as they witness the punishment of the offender. In the military style of group leadership, consequences are meant as punishments, not corrections. The culture of an organization or corps determines which type of leadership is most effective or desired. As one moves up through the ranks in the military from Private to General, leadership styles shift to a mixture of the two styles. More characteristics of relational leadership appear as rank increases.

What's the goal of leadership? The military's goal with new recruits is instilling a habit, a core allegiance to the mission, the organization, to fellow soldiers, and reflexive obedience. To accomplish this goal, the leadership style is by necessity (and name) purely militaristic.

All recruits don't graduate successfully from boot camp. The recruit changes when he begins living in a group experience. Boot camp teaches raw soldiers-in-the-making basic lessons of leadership and followership. For military purposes, for formulating and successfully waging war, it's imperative to direct a squad of men as a single unit. Anarchy in the ranks leads to casualties and defeat. Independence is death to the fighting man or woman.

How does one best lead a group of leaders?

How does one best lead a group of followers?

The simple rule, which begs for its many exceptions, is that leaders are led in a mix of military/relational leadership style, trending more toward the relational end of the continuum. Followers are also led by a mixture of the two styles, but trend more toward the militaristic end of the spectrum.

Followers want rules. They thrive on the security offered by boundaries and procedures. Rules offer consistency, reliability, clarity, and keep followers from feeling insecure and out of their depth. Rules offer comfort. This concept applies to children and horses also crave consistency and routine. Most people prefer consistency and security, with some more able than others to feel comfortable and secure in a routine of non-routine.

Leaders want the opportunity to step out in front and prove what they can do. They wilt and are repressed by too many boundaries and procedures. Leaders, by definition, must get out in front. Leading from behind creates pushers, changing the entire dynamic. It's been oft-repeated that, "God leads; Satan pushes." When considering the topic of leadership, this is a concept that effective Christian leaders must eventually contemplate.

How do you lead a group of leaders in an organization? The process of learning leadership and effective relationship skills is very similar. They're developed through trial and error, by experiencing success and failure. Like many skills or concepts, the greatest lessons often come after great failure. Leadership is a skill that generalizes to any situation, like relationship building. What do I mean by generalizing? If you learn to be an effective horse trainer, it means you can train almost any horse, regardless of breed, type, or disposition. Successfully training one horse does not a horse trainer make. Even someone who is famous for being an undesirable friend or coworker probably has one person with whom he has a successful relationship. He can't, however, replicate the result with other people. Horse trainers must be able to train many horses, not just one.

Leaders must be able to lead many types of followers in a variety of situations, not just one little group, one time. They must be able to replicate their leadership success. The same is true of relationship building.

Leadership is more complicated than simply looking at how a couple of basic styles work with different groups. Some leaders are placed in their positions by assuming the job within an existing group, like the incoming president of a club. The club members are there, the rules are in place, and hopefully the new president will be an effective leader. Being effective in this instance means fulfilling the mission of the club by utilizing the talents of the membership in ways that benefits the club and each member. The leader may steer the club in new and more productive directions to achieve higher levels of success. Proven leaders are necessary, even when an existing body is already somewhat orderly and effective. Otherwise the group will begin to weaken and factionalize. Poor leaders can wipe out the work done by prior excellent leaders unless action is taken to educate or remove them before the damage is irreversible.

There is a completely different leadership model that applies to leaders who attract and build a base of followership that didn't previously exist. These are unique people with uncommon skill sets. Most folks can learn leadership basics. However, not all people will be great leaders. I'll try to explain the difference using musical talent as an analogy.

In my family, any artistic musical talent went to my brother. Some ability for technical proficiency fell my way. My brother has perfect pitch, sings, can play an instrument by ear, and might have enjoyed some success as a musician. I can't carry a tune from one room to another, but I can read music and know how to translate little black dot on sheet music to finger position on a keyboard. For five years I was a bad organist for a little rural church. No one else stepped up to play, so the congregation was happy to have me, musical warts and all. Had I dedicated myself to a serious musical study I could have improved my skills, but no matter what I did, I could never have perfect pitch, sing with anyone but God benefiting, or play by ear. I didn't get the right ears.

What was the trade off? I learned that I could *lead*, that understanding the concepts of relationship building is part of my nature. My early career didn't always benefit from these skills. I had to learn basics, concepts, and how to apply them. Just as the person with perfect pitch feels a natural affinity to music, I feel a natural affinity for relational concepts. Training horses came naturally to me. But it took years of study, failures, successes, and many patient horses to develop skills that now generalize to almost any horse. The perspective I gained from being at the bottom of the stairs looking up in both relationships and groups, as well as that gained from the top of the stairs looking down, has been a vital tool for me. For instance, being a horse show judge taught me more about being a horse show exhibitor than any other single activity or study.

The View from the Center of the Arena

For years, I specialized in Halter horses. Fitting and showing halter horses is not the simple matter many believe it to be. It's nearly as complex as golf. Feeding and exercise programs for young horses often require daily tweaks to keep immature bodies healthy and growing normally. How high a horse holds its head when presented to the judge could be the difference between a first-place trophy and sixth-place ribbon. I'll never forget the first time I judged a halter class and saw an exhibitor bent over from the waist, backside facing me, resetting a front foot to present the horse better. All well and good, but not a pretty picture; the backside, I mean. I was mortified when I realized I'd made that exact move more than once. I never did it again.

Similar lessons came along by judging other events such as reining, pleasure, hunt seat, or trail. Seeing a performance from the center of the ring is totally different than watching it from the bleachers or in-gate. You can't properly judge unless you are the judge. There's a perspective that can't be shared with someone standing elsewhere in the arena or building.

On the other hand, I believe I was a successful judge because I was an exhibitor first. The evaluations I received as a judge were usually at the highest end of the scale. I became a judge to uniformly and fairly evaluate exhibitor performances by applying the rulebook and not by political or inappropriately subjective influence.

No one can learn all there is to know about horses or leadership. I suppose that's one reason natural horse trainers never hang up their snaffle-bit for good, and leaders never completely retire from people activities. There will always be higher goals and new lessons. The only way to test knowledge is to apply it.

Christians often have difficulty understanding leadership roles. Are we to judge others? In what circumstances and to

202

what degree? Where do we draw the line between brotherly love and accountability? There can be great confusion between the idea that "God will provide" and "I am responsible." Accountability is a fundamental element in both leadership and followership. Why do we have such difficulty requiring others to be accountable for their actions? When accountability is removed, leadership disappears, goals are not met, nations may crumble, and God is not served. Scripture never teaches us to be unaccountable. Several of Jesus Christ's parables speak specifically to accountability.

To sum up, when you lead groups you must determine which style of leadership will provide the best result. In most instances, you'll use a mixture of both the militaristic and relational styles. We must also develop a relationship with each horse we intend to use in a team. Once the relationship with each horse is well founded, we begin to work them together, each horse eventually learning to do its part of the whole.

God does the same with us. We work with the Spirit to build a right relationship with Him; His leadership being very relational and personal. He is a personal God. However, we all belong to a larger group as children of God, the body of Christ. We are all subject to the same rules and expectations, and as His children we will all be united in our final home— that place with many mansions that Jesus prepared for us.

DISTRACTIONS

Therefore keep watch, because you do not know the day or the hour
~ Matthew 25:13

If opportunity knocks while you are distracted—what was I saying?
~ Unknown

Have you watched horses or cattle spend late summer days in pasture, grazing on mature grasses, trying to search out one especially tender green shoot among the taller, tougher blades? If there is shelter available, horses and cattle mat spend much of the afternoon under cover or shoulder deep in the water, trying to avoid the hot sun and flies.

When flies are especially bad or the nastiest varieties make their way to the pasture, horse's bodies wear visual evidence of the tormentors. Horses with the thinnest skin are covered in welts ranging from the size of a mosquito bite to the size of a softball.

Just a few years ago, West Nile Virus became an issue for horse owners and humans. The virus is carried by mosquitoes with a high equine mortality rate, though less so for humans. Most well cared for horses are now vaccinated for West Nile

Virus as vigilant owners protect them from pestilence. Are you as concerned with the safety of your own family?

What books lurk in the back row of the bookcase upstairs in the junk room? What old videos hide in the box on your closet floor? What music is forgotten in the attic or stored on the iPod or MP3 players in your home? What magazines are concealed under your teenager's mattress? What websites do your children visit when they retire to their bedrooms for the night? Who do they chat with when you're not present?

What pests and varmints lurk in your home? In your spirit? Every wrong book, every wrong video, every wrong Internet search opens another portal for evil to enter your home and righteousness to leave. Does the way you dress matter? What you read? The music you listen to? What you watch on television? The answer to these questions is yes.

These are, at the very least, distractions from building a right relationship with God and, at worst, direct assaults by the enemy against the work of the Spirit. Until January 2008, I took the last few minutes before falling asleep to read the Bible and do my devotions. I struggled with my understanding, wondering if I needed special education. The truth is we all need special education and the good news is it's there for the taking. The question I should have asked myself is whether my difficulties were the result of inability or unwillingness. My answer probably would have been inability.

Now that I have been promoted to a higher grade, I know that what I kept stumbling over was unwillingness. For years, I indulged in intellectual pursuits of parapsychology, the spiritual, and reading about Christians who reported near-death experiences. I was never into anything other than pure discovery, learning more about God and where people fit into realms beyond our sight. I have the basic disposition of a researcher, so I figured I was being curious and thoughtful in this pursuit. In truth, my relationship with the Lord was handicapped by disobedience to His Word and the distractions and opportunities for evil that came in with my study materials.

God directly addresses this issue in His Word. Why I failed to grasp its meaning until then was a mystery, but it was finally revealed. Or maybe I'd finally cleared out enough distractions to properly diagnose my issue of unwillingness.

There is spiritual activity we can't see, but Christians are not to play in that arena. We are to inquire only of God, not the dead or spiritual beings who never had human form. Adam and Eve were told to stay away from the Tree of the Knowledge of Good and Evil. We are told to stay away from all sources of information outside the earthly realm other than those provided directly by the Lord for His purpose. Knowledge alone isn't virtuous, nor is all knowledge inherently healthy. The pursuit of forbidden knowledge adds to the mountain of distractions we must remove to find a right relationship with God. I had to learn to inquire only of the Lord for supernatural understanding and leave the rest alone.

Two things changed. The began to hear the quiet voice of the Spirit. I stopped giving the Lord the last little bit I had left every day and began giving Him the first and best of my day. Should this come as a surprise to any that we are to give the first fruits to the Lord? The concept of giving from what we have to the Lord debuts in Genesis chapter 4. My Bible has 2,624 pages of Scripture; this most basic element of right relationship appears on the ninth page. What does this mean to you about its relative importance?

The Lord looked with favor on Abel's offering, not so with Cain, who was sullen and unhappy about the situation. In Genesis 4:6–7, God asks Cain, "Why are you angry? Why is your face downcast? If you do what is right, will you not be accepted? But if you do not do what is right, sin is crouching at your door; it desires to have you, but you must master it." Well, you all know what happened next.

Finally figuring out (I didn't say I was a quick study) that I needed to give the beginning of each day to God rather than the remnant, the Spirit opened my eyes and ears to His teaching in exciting new ways.

The second thing that changed was recognizing the vulnerable openings I'd left for evil to inject distractions into my home. Every morning I prayed, read Oswald Chambers and the daily scripture. After these basics, I followed the Spirit's lead. One day I was pointedly reminded that a few books in the upstairs bookcase written by Christians reporting near-death experiences remained. I'd forgotten they were even up there. Talk about convicted!

I jumped up and flung every one of those books into the garage trashcan for pick up the next morning. I'd never waited so impatiently for the garbage truck. I ran through everything else I could think of that might possibly give opening to any spirit other than the holiest. Immediately the books were gone, I felt lighter in spirit than ever before. I returned to my chair, chastened and ashamed. My teacher had patiently waited for my return. He gave me a warm hug of approval and continued the day's lesson.

In the entry of our home is a sign quoting Joshua 24:15. "But as for me and my house, we will serve the Lord."

Nothing in our home can provide a stumbling block to that service. Not a television show, magazine, music, or even a catalog. Is it necessary to be so picky about what we allow into our homes? Does it bother you when one persistent fly keeps after you, landing first on your hand, then on your nose, then on your sandwich, then on your ear...? It drives you nuts!

Do you think God cares less about that one small, irritating object you refuse to part with than you do that tiny little fly? We allow many things in our lives that aren't evil, but they cause you way more work keeping distractions under control. Let me share a story from the barn. Maybe it will open your eyes to similar situations in your life and home.

When I fit halter horses in Arizona, I cooked them dessert each day. Oats boiled for two hours each afternoon. Once the oats and broth cooled, I added bran and dried molasses, stirring up the equivalent of a hot fudge sundae. The slop (as we called it) was the highlight of the horses' day. They nickered and begged until they could shove their eager faces down into their buckets of sweet oat soup. We called the warm mash slop because horses make the same noise happily smacking their way through their dessert as hogs in slop. The juicy mash created happy, sticky, pony faces.

We still cooked oats and served dessert in the cooler months after moving to Texas. It didn't take long before we began having a serious fly problem. The automatic fly system couldn't hold off the horde of annoying pests. I'd never experienced such a challenge. At that time, if I found three flies in my barn in one day, I prepared for war. There was just no keeping ahead of the flies. I couldn't figure it out. I resorted to using fly spray directly on the horses in the barn and unpacked flysheets and masks. I discovered that flies love slop. The molasses drew them like, well… flies.

We cleaned buckets daily, but just the remnant of soup kept them coming. Sadly, we quit cooking for the horses. The distraction isn't always a bad thing - quite the opposite, in fact. However, the extra work and annoyance caused by the flies exceeded the benefit, so slop is now a fond memory. I don't miss the extra work, but I do miss the delight my horses took in this wonderful treat. Nobody misses the flies.

Neighbors Are Part of Your Environment

Horse trainers try to control the environment as much as possible to reduce minor distractions caused by irritating flies or the greater problem of biting insects that break the concentration of the horse (and rider), making learning difficult or impossible. To keep our horses comfortable and able to learn, we need to prevent pests from invading our space. Flies and insects can be far more harmful than the obvious issues of nagging distraction. Horses will rub and scratch the itchy places caused by insect bites to the point of destroying manes and tails or opening cuts and sores trying to find relief.

Actual irritants and discomforts prevent horses from getting the most out of each lesson. On one hand, we limit the value of our training time if we allow flies to distract. On the other hand, not controlling mosquitoes can cause more than simple bites and rubs; mosquitoes can kill if they carry West Nile Virus.

Be mindful of distractions and varmints that affect you, your soul, and your family. It greatly matters with whom you associate and with whom your children spend their time. There are good influences and there are bad influences. There are environmental factors that are often dismissed as inconsequential when in fact they have great impact on your spiritual health. What do you allow in your home that offers the enemy a gateway?

You can no more keep your home in a proper condition for the Spirit to work efficiently than you can keep the hot summer winds from coming in through openings in poorly fitting doors and windows. Your air conditioner must work much harder to keep your house cool when it's not properly sealed than it would otherwise. The costs to you of drafty and poorly insulated homes are increased utility bills, less comfort, and a way bigger need to dust daily to remove the dirt blown in through cracks and crevices. The cost to you of unguarded access to your home and spirit-life is the degree to which you can be rightly related to God.

It absolutely matters with whom you associate, who your neighbors are, and what they do. You can keep the cleanest barn in the state, have a built-in fly system that regularly sprays your stalls and pens, serve feed-through products to your animals to kill larvae on manure piles, and even release fly predators to kill the ones you missed through your other efforts. However, if the guy next door has a horse, a cow, or a goat, and doesn't wage war against his flies to the same extent you do, his flies will be more than happy to visit your lovely place.

Many new horse owners asked me to suggest ways to control their fly problem. I always begin by asking about the neighborhood. Fly control is expensive. If your neighbor isn't concerned about his fly problem, you have a much shorter list of options for controlling yours.

Be Ruthless

What can you do? Be vigilant. Be aware. Be obedient. God will watch over you, your horses, and your family while you sleep. During the day, however, He expects you to seal the spiritual leaks in your home, monitor what is heard and seen by your family, and keep distractions to the lowest level possible. Be ruthless when clearing questionable material from your house.

Is this responsibility easy? No. Is it fair? The relationships you enjoy with your horse, your children, and with God are not democracies. These relationships are blessings. Horse owners strive to protect their horses from irritating and destructive pests. It's expensive, time consuming, and a constant battle from early spring till late fall. It takes planning and commitment. Would you do less for your home and family? For yourself?

Identify everything and anything that distracts you from the blessing of right relationship with the Lord. Remember, just one tiny fly can consume your attention. Open your home to God, but close it tightly against the distractions and filth of the enemy. Give God the first and best of your day. Clean house. Let the fresh, healing breezes of the Holy Spirit move into your home, your spirit, and your life.

CORRECTION, NOT PUNISHMENT

O Lord, correct me, but with judgment. ~ Jeremiah 10:24

Correction is not for the detection of faults, but in order to make perfect... Our wills must share in the making; God does not make us good in spite of ourselves. Those who take God's way of coming into the light will find, ultimately, nothing but unspeakable joy and peace, life and love. ~ Oswald Chambers

The differences that matter most between correction and punishment are ones of intent and goal. Punishment is used to confront; to dominate the one being punished. The goal of punishment is to stop an unwanted or dangerous behavior.

Correction is used to improve or make perfect. The goal of correction is encouraging right behavior. The visual picture of punishment and correction may look the same to the uninformed, but the one on the receiving end certainly knows the difference.

Some horses are cinchy; getting angry when the girth tightens around their belly. They don't react because the design of the saddle and girth are incorrect but because the hands that apply them are inept, arrogant, cruel, or ignorant.

213

Most horses learn to willingly accept metal bits and snug saddles when properly introduced.

Too often, trainers or horse owners resort to bigger bits or tighter girths to limit a horse's response or lock a poorly fitting saddle in place. Bigger bits are only properly used with increasingly lighter cues until the horse and rider move as one, with no visible method of communication. The pair appears to be united psychically, no longer tied to the merely physical. Severe bits or "enhanced training equipment" are (wrongly) used by trainers to dominate horses by inflicting pain when they want faster results or when owners exhaust their library of knowledge and resort to simple brutality.

On many occasions, I tied a horse's head around by a (snaffle) rein to the stirrup or girth ring. Was this punishment or correction? I used it as a way for the horse to teach itself. The rein was never so tight that the horse couldn't find the right answer and total comfort. My goal was teaching the horse to give to pressure. I haven't done this for quite a while now, as there are other methods I much prefer. However, when I had a whole string of horses to train, I couldn't spend as much time with each one as I am now. As a trainer, I was paid to get results. The horse's safety and welfare were of utmost concern, but if I could have one horse in the round pen teaching himself, I could be riding another horse in the adjacent arena, always keeping an eye on the one tied around.

Tying a horse around is a method of putting the horse in a bind until it figures the way out. This exercise must be done with judgment, wisdom, and under constant observation or it may quickly become an act of cruelty.

Have you ever found yourself in a bind? When the Lord puts us in a bind with judgment and wisdom, we can be sure we're never left unobserved. His plans always include the opportunity for us to find the answer that offers release. He may leave us to figure it out on our own for a time, but never in true peril. Horses remember lessons when they reasoned out the answer on their own. So do we.

Is there ever a circumstance where leaving a horse tied in a bind doesn't work? Absolutely. People don't all learn the same way and neither do horses. Few things are as frustrating to good horse trainers as horses who won't try. Put them into a bind, be it ever so slight, and they refuse to look for a way out. Pressure can be slowly and systematically increased to find the spot where the horse is motivated to find the way out of his problem. Some horses have no intermediate stop between ignore and explode. Good trainers know when to abandon the exercise and try another approach before the horse gets anywhere close to explode, exposing it to injury or worse.

Warning: never tie a rope or rein hard and fast to you or your horse unless you know what you are doing!

God must be totally frustrated with those who simply won't try. His subtle pressure is ignored. Instead of recognizing our situation, we persist in inaction until He is forced to change the program. His application of pressure, however slight, is meant to teach us. When we refuse to try, He may increase our bind slowly and methodically until we either learn or explode.

Unfortunately, many trainers and riders apply correction without wisdom or judgment.

The Noble Youth Horse

As a horse show judge, one of the rider errors that most irritated me occurred during youth trail classes. I can't count the number of times young riders banged their horses in the mouth with correction bits or jabbed them with sharp-roweled spurs when a trail obstacle was poorly performed. To be fair, there were plenty of adult riders in this group of bad actors. Memories flood my mind with instances where the exhibitor was an adult, or worse yet, a trainer, who "corrected" his horse in a similar way.

My frustration in these cases wasn't generated by the severity of the correction but the fact that correction was categorically unjustified. The poor performances weren't the result of a horse's refusal, confusion, sloppiness, or disobedience. My irritation was that in each instance, the horse obediently did exactly as the rider asked. The mistakes were 100 percent rider error, yet the poor horse was the one punished.

When I was a judge rulebooks didn't include specific rules penalizing such behavior. As a judge, I evaluated how well each obstacle was performed; judging correctness, style, and substance. I penalized riders every time they used their horse as a whipping boy, punishing poor horse when the rider deserved the blame. The pulling and poking applied by these kids never rose to the level of abuse, or I would have thrown them out of the arena. Nonetheless, these horses endured punishment for absolutely no good reason.

I can't tell you how many times I've said, "I have no idea why these horses don't just reach around to grab these kids, drop them in the dirt, stomp 'em, and walk away." Great youth horses take what the little monsters dish out without complaint. Do they refuse to retaliate out of fear or from nobility? It's hard to understand why an 1,100-pound animal would patiently submit to undeserved punishment for the bad behavior of the 95-pound kid on its back. Any time they wanted, these horses could ditch their kids and leave the arena. They never did.

I still feel respect, admiration, and affection for those wonderful youth horses. Only recently I noted the similarity of the behavior of these horses to the mortification of Jesus Christ. Jesus was sinless, yet He quietly endured punishment––unto death—for our bad behavior. At any time during His passion, Jesus could have ditched Pilate and the errant Jews and left the scene of His torment. He did not. How can we wrap our minds around such sacrifice? It wasn't fair. Again, the guilty (us) got off without punishment.

I don't know what causes youth horses to patiently endure punishment, not just for crimes they didn't commit, but enduring punishment applied by the very ones who are themselves guilty. The only explanation lies in the simplicity of horses. Like God, horses treat us exactly as we deserve - unless they bless us with grace.

Similar stories of horses receiving undeserved punishment in the name of correction repeat daily in the horse world. On behalf of all the horses and all my Christian brethren, I pray, as did Jeremiah, "O Lord, correct me, but with judgment."

Will every horse respond as hoped to judiciously applied correction? Correction that's appropriate, intended to improve, to make perfect, and done with a goal of encouraging the right behavior? Can we make every horse behave well despite its resistance? No, we can't. The horse's will is part of the equation and involved in the work of making perfect. Horses that learn to learn, that accept the trainer as a leader offering wonderful relationship, are the horses who find security and confidence, full mangers, warm stalls, and affection.

It's the same with Christians. We begin to respond to God; we accept Jesus Christ as our personal Savior who offers us relationship that surpasses our imagination. If we continue to experience correction, we know that we remain in training, still actively pursuing relationship with God. When we accept God's way, we come into the light, ultimately finding nothing but unspeakable joy and peace, life, and love.

I AM THE HORSE

I do what I don't will, and what I will I don't do. ~ Romans 7:19

God's commands are designed to guide you to life's very best. You will not obey Him, if you do not believe in Him and trust Him. You cannot believe Him if you do not love Him. You cannot love Him unless you know Him. ~ Dr. Henry Blackaby

Writing this, I realize how confusing the past two days have been. I've been ashamed and backslid in my walk with the Lord. I've been too independent in my work, as if I was becoming important in my own right again. Wrong!

Thankfully, I could go to the Lord. Ever faithful, He corrected me and gave me a way to finally understand what my role is and what it is not. God clarified for me – again - what I am to do and why. I needed to be slapped down and sent back into obedience training. The Lord was easier on me than I was on myself. He let me know I didn't sin, but did become somewhat untrained. Yet He welcomed me back and provided the moral to my lesson. When it comes to arrogance, I need regular maintenance.

Yesterday Baber and I took Copper and Bo to a mounted shooting competition. My work is taking more time than it did, and I've been devoting less regular time relationship with Bo and Swizzle. Trying to cheat our quality time...

Bo wasn't his usual obedient self at the event. There was a balloon crew, so we didn't need to run sticks. I missed the opportunity to refresh Bo's habit of obedience in that warm-up. Copper was okay, but stiffer than he needed to be and way too emotional, though not seriously. After two poor stages, with Bo offering some resistance and offering his opinion on what we should do, it became obvious that his habit of obedience needed maintenance.

Why in the world was Bo concerned about some rusty barrel in the trees a hundred feet away? Why did he throw his head up like a breathing statue because cattle moved lazily in the pasture on the other side of the road? When I first got on Copper, he refused to walk through a two-inch-deep depression. What? It took fifteen minutes of familiar exercises before Copper would go back and forth through the pitiful little rut in the road without hesitating or refusing. Take comfort, all you horse people. We all have days like this.

I could work both Bo and Copper through their disobedience because of our strong foundation. I lunged each with halter and lead rope at a trot, frequently asking them to turn from just the direction of my hand and a gentle feel in the lead. The familiar exercise transformed them from reactive to thinking, from independence to obedience. Our rides afterwards were exactly as they should be.

It occurred to me this morning that yesterday was really a lesson intended for me. Bo and Copper did to me what I'd done to God last week. In our routine at home, my grays remain obedient with little maintenance. It's easier for me as well to stay focused without the distractions of being out in public. Take me out to a "show", put me in another environment, especially one where I expect to shine, well, not so much. It took the trainer in me to recognize the issue with

Bo and Copper and work the fix. The trainer in me also recognized how I'd come untrained and what fix was necessary to correct my own behavior. Praise God I am blessed with these amazing horses.

In relationship with God, I am the horse; He is both owner and trainer, the best trainer. God knew me before He selected my parents, claimed me at birth, and cared for me every day of my life. He sent me out at the appropriate time for basic training. He has always been in total control of my program and any apprentice-trainer who worked with me was never left unsupervised. As I progressed and excelled, He sent me to practice shows and ultimately as a proven champion, though I've certainly never achieved champion status in His work.

Last October He brought me back to His barn. I came home to be His horse to be trained to do His work.

Just because I have a nice record as a show horse doesn't mean God will ever take me to show again. Only He knows if I'll ever perform for another's judgment again. This is not a waste of my talent or ability. He cares for me. I am only required to be obedient. The degree to which I commit to our relationship determines the degree to which I am elevated in His opinion and favor.

Yes, I look good with a full show clip, but such specific grooming is no longer important to Him. I don't have to be show ready to serve His purpose. He prefers me in a mostly natural state unless I'm to be slicked up to represent Him in an arena of His choice. I stay fit and healthy for my own benefit, but also to be ready whenever I may be called to work. Indeed, as a show horse I was clipped to exhibit a standard of appearance He may never choose again. In fact, I'm safer in most environments with some of my whiskers left in their natural state. He designed me well.

God provides a wonderful barn (home), beautiful pasture (community), and a circle of friends (my herd.) When He has no immediate need of me, I'm free to play, exercise, eat, relate to my herd, and make my own choices. I'm always to have an ear cocked in His direction, listening for His footsteps, waiting for His call. When God wants me, I want to be ready and come at the speed He requests. It's frustrating to ask a horse out in pasture to show up quickly and have to wait while it ambles in our general direction. When called, I don't want to keep Him waiting. That not the best way to begin a new assignment.

There's a lot of schooling left to do. Most of my training is done at home in private. He takes me out to test our relationship to determine how well I've learned my lessons. My skills are to be available to Him at the time and place of His choosing. God keeps me maintained; faithful to provide fine tuning when needed for more precise tasks.

At times, I may be used as a leader to show a more timid horse the way, or as a pony horse to guide another in a loose partnership, but always directed by my Leader. God chooses when, He chooses whom, and He chooses where. I'm no longer a full-time show horse. I'm still capable, but that's not His plan as far as I see it. Today I am the beloved friend, companion, partner, and obedient horse of a Master who promises to value and cherish me forever.

Relationship is all that truly matters. Everything else is merely window dressing.

PRETTY IS AS PRETTY DOES

He had no beauty or majesty to attract us to him, nothing in his appearance that we should desire him. He was despised and rejected by men. ~ Isaiah 53:2-3

Do you love me because I'm beautiful, or am I beautiful because you love me? ~ Oscar Hammerstein II

Susan Boyle isn't a beauty by any traditional standards. But at 47, she stunned the world in April 2009 in a British talent competition with her rendition of "I Dreamed a Dream" from *Les Miserables.* The three-judge panel was first highly skeptical, then enraptured, when she opened her mouth and the beauty of her song filled the theatre.

How many people are outwardly beautiful yet inwardly corrupt? How can such beauty, talent, innocence, even naiveté, reside in a woman who looked like Susan Boyle at her audition?

How does our world view a Susan Boyle? It depends on what eyes are used to see her. If we use the eyes of a corrupted people, we discount Susan's gift; seeing little beauty. Indeed, we wish her to leave the stage so someone more attractive than she may can enter the spotlight. With such ignorant eyes, we are repulsed by the unexpected contrast between the physical and the vocal, demanding that someone more acceptable replace this one. That's what happened.

However, if we look with eyes of righteousness, with eyes still able to see what lies beneath the veneer, we are elevated by Susan Boyle's gift. Not only her song, but also her innocence. She is captivating. How could such talent hide for so many years? Susan lived a life of service to her parents. She never attempted to venture into the limelight until this competition.

Today, the greater part of value is in the physical; in youth, in celebrity, in all that fades and is but dust when we pass on. What's wrong with us? When we first discovered Susan Boyle I asked a friend of mine what she would choose, if she had the opportunity to receive Susan's gift but would also have Susan's appearance. Would she choose beauty of face and form or amazing beauty of spirit and song? I was surprised that my friend answered without hesitation; she would accept the physical to obtain the spiritual. Mind you, my friend is a very attractive lady. If I asked myself the same question, what answer would I give? I don't know. What would you choose?

While I'm not inclined to exchange my life for anyone else's, I could use a bit of introspection in how I conduct my own. Why am I concerned about the wrinkles spreading across my face? Why do photographs from twenty or thirty years ago make me feel like I'm somehow failing because I don't look the same?

Any meaningful beauty I can offer won't be physical. The only true beauty is the spiritual beauty given to me through relationship with Jesus Christ. Such beauty is only visible to others if I'm oblivious to it. There's the difficulty. I know that. I want spiritual beauty. I also want physical beauty. I was used to having it. So, what's the bottom line?

I want to be obedient to the Lord. I can only enjoy the relationship I want with Him by willingly losing myself and becoming what the Spirit can make me. What lesson can we learn from Susan Boyle? The sensation she caused is due to marrying her childlike affect to the phenomenal beauty of her song, which is in such stark contrast to her appearance. What happened? Her appearance began to assume the beauty of her inner radiance. Will she agree to a complete makeover of the external? Would a makeover lessen the package? God brought her to this place. May she remain true to the beauty she came with. May God's Spirit give me inner beauty to transform my aging exterior like Susan's.

You Can't Ride Beauty

Most horse trade publications contain articles on the state of the economy, specifically horse markets and related industries. An emerging direction in horse values favors horses with good job skills. Horse values have always revolved around three corners of the market triangle: potential, appearance, and utility. The relative weight of each change rapidly when economic realities and markets shift. For years, market demand drove the value of potential to increasingly higher levels as breeding numbers increased and the price of good, then great, broodmares and yearlings skyrocketed. Potential was king of the marketplace, bringing the dominant share of auction bids.

There's always been good value with proven winners, but the older the horse, the smaller the pool of interested buyers. Once a performance horse exceeds the age of nomination or eligibility to major money competitions, its value nosedives. In the casual riders market, young never had the value-added status it did in the performance horse market, so it's no surprise that values for mature casual market horses remained steady but never reached the fever pitch of the cutting, reining, western pleasure and racing markets. Beauty and potential were hot sellers. What is selling today?

The potential corner of the market triangle isn't bringing the return it did just a couple of years ago. Thankfully, breeding numbers are going down as market demand ebbs. Increasing value is being placed on seasoned horses well established in their occupations, whether casual riding, roping, barrels, competitive trail, or other. Dressage and eventing communities have long placed a high value on maturity and proven ability. The high-selling horse at a recent horse sale owned and managed by a well-respected and successful auction company was an unregistered palomino pony, well-seasoned in ranch work and taking care of children. That pony sold for more than many yearling colts, who just a couple of years ago would have sold for twenty times what the pony did. Potential isn't king of the auction ring anymore.

Beauty is indeed in the eye of the beholder. If you looked for a mount for your five-year-old granddaughter, would you choose the flashy five-year-old pony that still has obedience issues or the faithful and patient fifteen-year-old pony that isn't much of a looker? I hope you'd take the fifteen-year-old home to a comfy stall and eager granddaughter. Once that pony and your granddaughter establish relationship, that plain little pony will become the most beautiful horse on God's earth.

Spirit transforms us from the inside. This is what relationship with God is all about. So, what do we learn from Susan Boyle? I learned that I would rather be the plain old pony, beloved by my mistress, than the flashy pony not yet fit for right relationship with any master. As the plain old pony, I'm assured of a loving, permanent home where Spirit eyes clearly see my beauty.

RELATIONSHIP, THE GREATEST BLESSING

The Lord is my light and my salvation. One thing I have desired of the Lord, that will I seek: that I may dwell in the house of the Lord all the days of my life. ~ Psalm 27:1,4

Life is relationships; the rest is just details. ~ Dr. Gary Smalley

When we sold our ranch, we built a new house and much smaller horse set-up on one of our hayfields. For the first time in many years, we can see everything we own from anywhere on the place. There are no remote fields to hay a mile from the house or cattle grazing in a pasture out of sight of the main buildings. The new barn is so close we can see our way to the door of the tack room after dark just by turning on the back-porch light.

Over the years, I've built show barns and barns used mostly for foaling. I've remodeled barns and designed barns from scratch. This is the first time I designed a barn strictly for our personal horses. This barn won't house horses coming in for training, boarding, or foaling. It's just for our little herd.

Convenience and comfort were my primary considerations in the design. Well, economy was also involved, as this barn was pure expense and not a business investment. But I still wanted my horses housed in a light, airy environment where they have easy access to each other, simple but adequate feed storage, a big enough tack room without being expansive, and completely covered, attached runs so we never have to clean manure out of the mud again. (At least, that was the plan.) The back of each horse's stall/pen combo opens directly into the big back pasture.

In addition to ease of use, one of my highest priorities for the whole place was *low maintenance*. We are not as young as we were, and I have little interest in stuff. All we've been blessed with has the responsibility of good stewardship attached. "To whom much is given, much is required." We've been divesting ourselves of stuff for years. My rule for stuff is, "If I don't need it or I don't love it, I don't want it."

My horses are pets for the first time in twenty years. During most of my equine career, horses were breeding stock, bred to sell, owned by clients, or horses purchased for eventual resale. Even the few I claimed as my own weren't really pets. They all had jobs and a purpose. I didn't have time to develop the depth of relationship with any of them that I have now. I've always loved horses, but horses became my job. Just like that proverbial cobbler who had no time to make shoes for his own children, I didn't have time to concentrate on my own horses. As a trainer, my loyalty was to my clients. Occasionally, I had to leave our horses at home when we traveled to a horse show, knowing that my horse would likely place higher than a client's horse. That would have been a bit messy and not very professional.

Chili Bean

Sometimes we don't know what we have until we lose it. Sometimes we don't realize what we don't have until we find it. This story is like the latter. Six months before we moved off the ranch to our new place, I lost my dog. Chili Bean was my baby for fifteen years. Chili, a red miniature dachshund, was one of the special ones. She understood English, and our relationship was a total blessing to me. Chili was my most faithful and understanding companion in every situation, even protecting our belongings one night at a major horse show when thieves raided the tack rooms. Little Chili was a true dachshund in many ways, an avid hunter and ready to defend her family's stuff. The special horses and special dogs that bless our lives know our thoughts before we do and happily give us 110 percent of themselves. Chili was more than a dog. It was difficult to lose her. If you've been through a similar situation, you know how I felt.

For weeks, each day started with the same question, "Is this the day?" Chili was increasingly unable to find a comfortable position. We gave her pain medication and steroids, but she continued to deteriorate. Finally, the medication wasn't enough. Chili was constantly in pain. The dreaded day arrived. When I returned from the veterinarian's office, I entered the house alone. I wasn't prepared for the void created by Chili's absence. We still had four dogs in the house, yet the life had somehow gone out of it. The heart of my home stopped beating. My home was now only a house.

My husband mourned Chili's loss deeply. God was still on His throne. Yet, I had no home, just a house. No horse in the barn would understand if I woefully hugged its neck. None of our other dogs could comfort me. Baber understood; he's an amazing critter daddy, but he's an autonomous adult. He doesn't need me to make a home for him. I'd never experienced this before. My beloved dachshund-child, Snooker, passed away in 1990. Snooker deserves a story all her own, but not here. Her passing was worse than Chili's in some ways, but when Snooker passed away, I did have a horse in the barn willing and able to provide the comfort I needed. That horse and I had a

229

relationship that reassured me I was still needed to make him a home.

It is only now, as I write this, that I understand the process of these losses. There can be dry periods in our lives, devoid of those rich, special relationships. The empty place remains until another relationship fills it. God only explains this to us in hindsight. It's comforting knowing that He has a plan. We can't understand the plan as it unfolds, but He'll faithfully bring understanding at the proper time.

The first morning without Chili was quiet. There was still no heartbeat in the house. What an odd situation. No one needed me to make a home. The sense of abandonment and uselessness was like sensory deprivation, where ties to reality are shredded. I had no problem with reality but felt adrift without a firm tether to home. That condition continued until yesterday.

Love Was Born in a Stable

As the Lord walked me through the work of this book, He expanded my understanding of the relationships I have both with Him and with my horses. The blessing of relationship with Jesus Christ is the foundation of my soul and the joy of my life. I am blessed with a husband with whom I am evenly yoked, the freedom to live as we like, and family and friends we hold dear. I thought no greater blessing was possible - at least as far as earthly relationships go.

Yesterday began as a beautiful spring day in north central Texas - sunny, breezy, and warm. Baber and I went out to the barn after finishing our inside chores and study. We curried more shedding hair off the horses. I groomed Bo and Swizzle while he groomed Copper and Asti. We saddled all four and enjoyed wonderful rides. The clear, sunny day was one of the perfect ones. All four horses learned something new in their lessons, as did we. When the horses were brushed and turned back out to pasture, Baber and I headed off separately to do other projects.

As is typical in north central Texas weather, this spring day that began with brilliant sun and warm breezes quickly changed. The wind began to howl - I mean at gale force levels. The sun was replaced with thick, dark clouds, and the warm balmy day was fast becoming a cold, gusty, winter evening. Temperatures were expected to drop below freezing. Late in the afternoon I went to the barn. Temperatures were already in the low forties with winds gusting to forty miles per hour. As soon as the horses saw me leave the house, they galloped to the barn and wanted into their stalls! I asked them to be patient while I added fresh shavings to each stall, checked waterers, and placed large flakes of grass hay into each feeder. Even though the four horses desperately wanted in, they entered their houses in orderly fashion, being just as polite and as patient as expected.

The wind howled as temperature continued to fall. The horses were so happy to be inside. They were well into the shedding process, so I debated whether to put blankets on them. The three older horses hadn't worn a blanket in the two years since we moved, becoming semi-pasture horses. Swizzle, the youngest, had never worn a blanket.

I made my decision. My horses would not be cold. Sure, they could take the cold; they were in the barn. But they are precious to me, and I am responsible for their care and delighted to make them secure and comfortable. Out came the blankets. I had to vigorously brush up one or two to get two years of dust off. Clean blankets are folded and stored neatly in sealed plastic bags, but these blankets were worn a few times right before we moved and not cleaned and bagged, just folded in the tack room. They'd never been wet or dirty, just dusty where the odd end or strap was exposed.

The three older horses eagerly ducked their heads into the neck openings of their blankets. Swizzle had never worn a

231

blanket, and the one I had for her had no opening at the front, so the only way to get it on her was over her head. She only needed a few minutes to learn about clothes. Once all four were tucked cozily into their jammies and clean, fresh stalls, I went back to the house. At dinner time, I went to the barn to give my little ponies a big flake of alfalfa hay, picked their stalls, and made sure the blankets were all still in place. All was quiet, peaceful, and strangely satisfying.

The next morning was the opposite of that first morning without Chili. Somehow my joy expanded beyond normal limits. I felt greatly blessed. Life seemed bigger today than it was yesterday. What happened?

The blessing of relationship. I was needed again as a homemaker. My grays stepped up to more than meet me halfway in our relationship. The absolute delight I felt preparing the barn to ensure the comfort and safety of my horses was totally unexpected. My home had a heartbeat again! Love was born, again, in a stable.

My limited writing skills don't allow me to describe what such relationship means. I know God used this experience as both a blessing and lesson for me. Our lives can go along in an orderly, contented manner, without even knowing what we're missing without such relationships. Once we experience them, we're never truly satisfied until we find them again.

God created us to be in relationship with Him. Part of our souls, our hearts, remains empty unless filled with Him. No other relationship can take the place reserved for God alone. Once you taste relationship with Him the empty place begins to fill. In John 14, Jesus promises to prepare a place just for us. There's a place with your name on it today, and relationship with Jesus Christ that will forever fill that empty place. He prepared a place just for you when you go home to Him. I know the joy I received preparing a place for Bo and Swizzle. Imagine how much more Jesus did in the place He prepared exclusively for you.

PROGRESSIVE RELATIONSHIP

Because you have kept my command to persevere, I also will keep you from the hour of trial, which shall come upon the whole world. ~ Revelation 3:10

This is the humanist dilemma. They say, "You come from nothing and you're going to nothing, but in between you have great significance." It doesn't make sense at all. ~ Pastor Ray Pritchard

The pressure and correction the good trainer applies to her horse is never an element of the lesson but the result of the horse's failure to comply with, or obey, a request or expectation. Oswald Chambers writes of a similar circumstance Israel found itself chronicled in the book of Jeremiah. He wrote, "the prophet realizes that the sufferings and the judgments that are about to fall on the people of God are not a Divine edict, but the result of that people's revolt." In other words, they brought it all on themselves.

Our desire for self-realization is the enemy of relationship with God. Similarly, a horse's desire to remain outside of accountable relationship with the trainer becomes the enemy to the success of the relationship. Taken to its ultimate end, the relationship terminates.

As it is between trainer and horse, so it is between God and man. All the worldly voices preaching self-love, turning away from God, are the enemy of right relationship. The prevailing message in media and throughout much of society is the worship of humanity.

How do we know if we're experiencing the blessing of a right relationship with God? The symbol of the Holy Spirit is fire. The progressive relationship we have with God is frequently described as a "consuming fire" or a "refining fire."

The difference between God as a consuming fire and natural fire is just this, that the further you get away from God the more fiercely you feel His burnings, but when you are close to Him, you will find it (the fire) a glorious protection. ~ Oswald Chambers

The same is true as we train and build relationship with a horse. One of the first lessons we teach our horse is that safety and security is found near us. There is no pressure when the horse is close to us, yet respectful of our personal space. As the horse leaves our side and then returns, he begins to understand that pressure and predicament occur when he chooses to leave without our specific direction. Once the horse returns, it finds glorious protection.

Relationships are either progressive or regressive. There's no such thing as a static relationship between living things. A trainer can never reach a desired level of relationship with her horse, rest on her laurels, and expect the relationship to continue at the same level. The moment a lesson is learned or a new height of relationship achieved, the process of maintenance begins. Unless the relationship continues to progress, building upon the existing foundation, the connection begins to deteriorate. Maintenance is necessary for any lesson, concept, or skill we don't practice regularly.

Perhaps you worked for weeks or months to build a relationship with your horse and in the process taught it to bow. Excellent. With this success in your pocket you move on to master more skills as you continue building relationship. Then you become fascinated with a new type of competition. In the process teaching the new maneuvers, building confidence that you and your horse can successfully compete in the new event, you stopped practicing the bow. After all, your horse already knows that trick.

By focusing on other lessons, your horse's ability to perform the perfect bow on cue gradually begins to erode. One day you want to a new friend how well your horse bows. You give the cue and... nothing happens. Without regular maintenance, every skill gets rusty and eventually disappears. A refresher course will get your horse bowing again. You've learned to include maintenance of desired skills to your training calendar.

Our relationship with God either progresses – with deeper commitment and shared experience - or regresses. Occasional maintenance won't keep this relationship shiny. Progressive relationship with God brings vitality, security, peace, joy, and new spiritual insights. Only when nearest to God may we enjoy His glorious protection.

Sometimes trainers reach a level of relationship with a horse that they find satisfactory, but if another horse with greater promise comes along, the first is turned out to pasture. The retired horse will receive excellent care, green pasture, and clean water. It will want for nothing, except relationship with the trainer. There may be other horses for company, but what made that horse special was removed.

Christians can be saved, yet find themselves turned out to pasture. If we don't continue building relationship with God, expanding the places where His fire protects us, we may find ourselves locked out of the barn. We will be saved, but we've lost the special place we might have had by continuing in progressive relationship with the Lord.

Progress is only made, whether man or horse, by continuing obedience. Are you progressing in your relationship to the Lord, or content to slip away to do your own thing? Anyone telling you that the moment you're saved is the end of the journey works for the other side. Once you recognize a need for a relationship with Jesus Christ, you've only established a beginning.

ABANDONMENT

The Lord is the strength of my life; of whom shall I be afraid? ~ Psalm 27:1

God has great things in store for His people; they ought to have large expectations. ~ C.H. Spurgeon

Are you ready to let God lead you into full union with Him, abandoning your right to yourself, and becoming fully obedient to His direction? Will you release the strings you clutch ever more tightly in the desperate attempt to keep balloons filled with your dreams from floating away? When you abandon to God, you stop asking questions. You trust Him. As soon as you fling off independence you receive freedom unlike anything you ever dreamed of. You will own the elusive joy and peace you've heard about but never understood.

You are not lost in abandonment; you are found. There isn't any maybe or if; you know whether you're in a right relationship with God. Not a perfect relationship, but a right relationship. If not, it's because you withhold either obedience or trust from the Lord.

How many of us trust God to handle our affairs for today and the future? Our nature is to get independent and pushy. What we're really doing is limiting what's possible by restricting what we allow God to do with us. The only way to remove the ceiling from what is possible and discover options we never dreamed of is to abandon to God.

It's been said that the journey of a thousand miles begins with a single step. Without a specific destination in mind, we think we can't take the first step. If I don't know where I am going, should my first step be to the north, south, east, or west? If you feel you must move from the spot you're presently rooted to, just take a step. Pick any direction. When Jesus performed healing miracles, He didn't just wave a hand. Jesus required action from the one about to be healed. Jesus said, "Stretch out your hand," or, "Arise and take up your bed." Jesus didn't lower Himself to the sinners' level; He asked sinners to raise themselves to where He was and then "sin no more."

By focusing on the Lord, you slowly begin to see where your next step should be, then another, and so on. You'll never get anywhere else if you don't go somewhere *else*. To change something, you must change *something*. It seems obvious, but we forget what we know in the confusion and complexity we create in our lives.

You can't train a horse without movement. You can't teach a horse to turn left unless he's moving forward. You can't teach a horse to stop unless it's already in motion. Highly trained horses often move in highly collected frames. That means they expend greater energy and perform more difficult maneuvers by more specifically controlling their muscles rather than increasing speed.

It's counterintuitive to apply more gas to go slower. That's the product of collection. Highly collected movements are very difficult. The horse's mind is conditioned as well as its body. Muscles gradually strengthened over time allow horses to maintain collected frames for an extended period. The most advanced horses can make such exertion look easy. Christians go through a similar training program, learning over time to perform in closer unity with God, where the greatest works look like the least.

Limitless Vision

If the highest achievement we envision with our horse is riding safely on a familiar trail then that becomes the limit of our reach. By pursuing a relationship with our horse with specific goals in mind and the dedication to provide trustworthy and wise leadership, we enable our horse to rise above the restrictions of its prey nature.

There will be times when the blossoming relationship between you and your horse offers revelations about your role as a child of God. At other times the Holy Spirit may reveal a biblical truth, solving a nagging problem you were fruitlessly trying to work out with your horse—or your child. Through relationship with us, horses achieve greater levels of performance than what is possibly naturally, just as God expands ours. Only in abandonment can our eyes see light where only darkness existed before.

No one has ever found a limit to what the horse-human partnership can accomplish. Most of us lose our way by concentrating on the goal of task and not depth of relationship. We narrow our focus, seeing only with tunnel vision. Are focus and commitment required to achieve goals? Absolutely. The issue is what we focus on and what goals we set. My point is that we set unnecessary limits on what is possible by focusing on goals using only our own intellect and vision. God's vision is limitless.

Abandonment to God offers delight, emotions, experiences, and insights not possible by other means. A double blessing is receiving all these benefits with married a deep security of personal safety. We shelter in the shadow of

His wing and rise above danger by resting in the palm of His hand. We learn to trust with the simplicity of a child.

Is a four-year-old child concerned and depressed because the Russians are presenting a more aggressive military posture? No. The child isn't concerned about those big issues; mom and dad take care of all that stuff. Most big issues register to children. Jesus tells us to become as little children, abandoning our cares and concerns to the Lord. Little children are expected to play fair, share, and pick up their toys. Responsibility is appropriate to their position and maturity. When it comes to relationship with God, it's no different. Expectations and responsibilities just look a little different.

Let's examine this concept from the trainer-horse perspective. What does abandonment look like? The horse who abandons to the trainer asks no more "why" questions. The relationship the trainer creates firmly establishes the habit of obedience. Horses love routine, concerned mainly with food, water, shelter, rest, and relationship with herd mates. Horses play and are inquisitive. Some horses have low boredom thresholds; some are stodgy and a bit obtuse, but all horses must have a leader to feel secure. Are we much different?

When a horse enters training, it has no idea of the possibilities that lie ahead. The trainer knows the basic plan, but the horse must work through each successive lesson and step before the next opportunity is presented. Exposing a horse to a concept too far above its experience results in failure, perhaps injury, and may ruin the horse's chance of eventually mastering the concept. Such outcomes are the result of leadership failure. People react in much the same way.

As our horse becomes obedient in small things, we discover it's now safe and secure on a simple neighborhood trail ride. Any issue that arises is handled by additional training and building sturdier foundations. As new levels of performance and trust build, we compete in a novice rail class and maybe a walk-jog trail class. If we perform well, testing our horse's obedience and concentration, we either succeed or identify areas requiring attention. We don't measure our horse's success by the judge's opinion, but by the obedience, the abandonment, of the horse to our direction. You probably know what happens when a horse decides it wants a democratic relationship; insisting on a vote before engaging in an activity or maneuver. My horses and I are a team, but there's no confusion about who leads.

I will, however, ask my horse to step up and make independent decisions. Without allowing our horses the opportunity to lead they can't develop confidence in their ability to do all the things we want to enjoy with them. Confidence is important and built by successful experience. Self-confidence allows us to take risks. The greater our confidence, the greater the risks we're willing to take. The more confidence my horse has in me and in us, the more willing he is to step out and perform a maneuver he considers risky. Obedience and confidence motivates him to try. Avoiding problems never develops confidence; facing and resolving problems does.

As horse and trainer work through stages leading to complete abandonment, possibilities explode. The horse that was afraid to get into a horse trailer or jump a fallen log becomes a horse able to compete in the Olympic Games in a distant country.

Do you really think humans are more limited in possibility than horses? As we abandon more to God, what is possible for us also explodes. Ship that never break connection to the pier never begin a voyage, much less complete one. We can't explore what's possible and soar to greater heights if we're unwilling to release the strings that tether us to the limits of our own narrow vision.

I love this illustration of abandonment from Guillaume Appollinaire, a turn-of-the-century Polish poet and philosopher:

"Come to the edge."

"We can't. We're afraid."

"Come to the edge."

"We can't. We will fall."

"Come to the edge."

And they came.

And he pushed them.

And they flew.

Only in abandonment to God are we certain to never be abandoned. Are you abandoned to God?

THE SPOTTED WONDER

God's finger touched him, and he slept. ~ Alfred, Lord Tennyson

Yesterday would have been his eighteenth birthday. I was there when he was born, hands cradling his beautiful head as he took his first breath. I was there, touching his cheek, when he drew his last breath before returning to his Maker. Rarely do I shed tears, but they're about spill - and I'm only writing the first paragraph.

They are tears of failure and waste - two things I never wanted to be guilty of. But there it is. Most of *Amazing Grays, Amazing Grace* deals with the successes and enjoyment of life with Bo and Swizzle and how relationships with other horses over the past two decades helped me better understand my relationship with God. The story of my Spotted Wonder ends this book and may give you hope as you move forward in your relationships with humans, with horses, and with God.

You wouldn't be get the whole story if I left out the part where God blessed me with the specific answer to prayer - and I squandered it. I am profoundly ashamed that I didn't understand the consequences of choices made so many years ago. Yet, I am equally thankful that although that door is forever closed, I did learn the lesson it provided. God never seems to run out of lessons, and He never runs out of grace.

A couple of years into my horse career we eagerly awaited the birth of our first foal. After weeks of careful watching, he arrived at two thirty in the morning. My friend Jackie and I sat in lawn chairs in the breezeway of our mare motel. She had been present when hundreds of foals entered the world.

As Sugar strained through each contraction, the miracle began. First came tiny striped hooves, slippered with thick, golden "gelatin" that allows easy passage through the birth canal. Then a tiny dark head with a brilliant white blaze, the little tongue already out and cupped; brown shoulders; and then the most perfect snow-white blanket with spots beginning halfway down the foal's back and finishing where well-muscled haunches met the hind legs. It was a boy, a perfect little stud colt.

For me, it was love at first sight. Sugar, who'd already done this several times, wasn't as excited. She rolled up onto her chest and groaned. Over the years, I learned that Sugar was perfectly content to deliver her foal then pass its care to me. Sugar was a good mama, but didn't want to get too involved until she'd gotten some rest and the hot bran mash she came to expect. For Sugar, it was food first, take care of the kid later.

The colt wallowed about like a water spiker for the first twenty minutes. Once his legs gathered strength and he gained control of them he popped up. By then I'd already toweled him dry, stroked his soft coat countless times, and decided he would be my horse forever. This was the horse I'd always wanted. That special one. He didn't disappoint in any way. He was an answer to prayer.

All went well; or so we thought.

One of the most nerve-racking parts of foaling is being sure the foal gets the first milk, the colostrum. It's loaded with antibodies to protect the foal as well as sealing the GI tract and helping to pass the meconium. Once a foal is delivered you wait for the placenta to pass completely and for it to stand and nurse. Some foals figure out where the milk is and how to get it long before others. This colt was born with his tongue already out, cupped and ready to put his natural suck reflex to work. Soon he was looking around for a place to put his tongue to good use. Sugar was not impressed. She had a bellyache, but she dutifully cocked a hind leg to make access easier for him.

That tongue was all over. First it got covered in hair looking in the wrong place. I cleaned it off. Was this colt an idiot? How long was it going to take him to find the milk? He was a strong colt with straight legs and a big personality. But gracious, he was slow finding breakfast. Eventually he got in the right position and worked his tongue all over Sugar's bag. She had plenty of milk and the stimulation of the colt's attempts caused her to squirt milk out all over. Finally, we heard that good suck sound, got under Sugar from the opposite side, and verified that the colt was indeed nursing. Sugar cleaned out well, and it was time for Jackie and me to head in. Dawn was breaking. I was exhilarated, but tired.

I went out to see my beautiful colt the moment I woke up. His head was covered in sticky milk, evidence he'd been under Sugar regularly. I got a bucket of warm water and washcloth and cleaned him up. He loved the attention. I watched to make sure he got busy in the milk department again. I heard sucking sounds then headed to the feed store with Jackie.

After a celebratory lunch, we got back mid-afternoon. Our first stop was the nursery. Something didn't seem right. The colt didn't look quite as strong, and Sugar rebuffed his attempts to get under her to nurse. Sugar wanted nothing to do with him, driving him away when he tried to nurse. His head was covered in dried sticky milk again. I checked Sugar's nipples. They had not been nursed on! His tongue made the right sounds on her bag but he wasn't getting any milk. He was dehydrated and needed attention. We put a halter on Sugar and tried to get the baby over to nurse. He went, he looked, he sucked, but he didn't know how to get the nipples to work. He gamely kept his dry little tongue cupped but never got it right.

My veterinarian came almost immediately. We milked Sugar so Dr. Madia could tube it into the baby. We made sure the colt had adequate fluids and was strong enough to leave at home. He was. He always would be. The vet gave instructions to try to get him to nurse regularly and bottle feed him a few ounces of milk every few hours if necessary. Not too much, because he would stop looking if he felt satisfied. Even with this rocky beginning, the veterinarian asked if he was for sale. I didn't think so, but I asked why the interest so soon. Dr. Madia said that many people wait a lifetime for a colt like mine and never get one. This foal was special. He thought so, and so did I.

Once her bag was milked down, Sugar was more comfortable but still not too happy with her dumb kid. She figured that if he was too stupid to nurse, he should be my responsibility, not hers. Since that was an unacceptable response, Jackie and I took turns teaching the colt remedial nursing. First, she would hold Sugar, requiring her to stand quietly (even if not patiently) while I tried to guide the baby's tongue to the right place. When I failed, we changed places. He always got there but just didn't get the suck thing right.

Getting out the nipple and bottle the vet left, I milked Sugar into a yellow plastic, four-cup mixing bowl and poured the thick, sticky milk into a soft, plastic bottle. If you've never milked a mare, I can tell you it's not easy. You strip each nipple just like a cow, but the nipple is only about one-inch

246

long and the milk only comes out with a gentle pull. My present vet has perfected a method of milking mares more efficiently, but I didn't know how to do that all those years ago. I found that warm, wet fingers work the best for milking mares. I used that same yellow mixing bowl and bottle many times over the next twenty years.

Once I had two or three ounces of milk in the bottle, I attached the lamb nipple and offered it to the colt. He recognized the smell and was interested right away. I wiggled one finger in the corner of his mouth to open it. Of course, that little tongue was still out and cupped. I lay the nipple in the curl of his tongue, tilted his head up, and let a few drops of milk slide into his mouth. Then I let a few more drops dribble in. The colt shook his head out of my hand, swallowed, and then came looking for more. I put the nipple back into the curl of his tongue; he laid his tongue around the nipple, made a solid connection, and...sucked! He swallowed the entire bottle in about two seconds. We have suck!

The first swallow of warm milk was what the poor baby had been working for since his tongue first made connection with air. He was born with his tongue sticking out in suck position, and he'd finally gotten the job done. He wanted more! Of course, he figured I was the source of the milk, and followed me around the pen asking for more. It was time to put Sugar back into the equation. Jackie and I set up again, she holding Sugar and me trying to get the now motivated colt into nursing position. I used the milky nipple to lead his nose to Sugar's udder.

When I finally got his tongue on the nipple, the connection was made and nature took over. After one more head-washing session to get the milk off his face and a few more conversations with Sugar, the saga came to a wonderful end and we never had a medical issue with this colt again that wasn't directly caused by a human.

We came frighteningly close to losing this first foal. I never again took a chance on whether a new foal nursed correctly. I generally give a baby about an hour to figure out how to nurse. After that I milked mama and bottle-fed the baby its first course. Some foals needed to be bottle fee-d (or even syringe fed) for days until they were strong enough or coordinated enough to nurse on their own.

We named our beautiful colt Abduls Bright Sky, "Sky" for short. Annoyingly, several of the colts he sired were a bit slow to nurse correctly, just like daddy. His fillies were smarter. Isn't nature interesting?

Sky had the most engaging personality. He loved people, even kids. Sky was smart. Sky was gorgeous. Sky was a miracle. He was the answer to my prayer. He would be my horse. Whatever I expected of him, he was always more.

Time passed. Sky was weaned and given his own stall and pen. He quickly learned everything I taught him. He was nearly perfect. Perfect color, head, legs, muscling, disposition, pedigree, conformation, everything. Sky was born to be a stallion. Wasn't I the luckiest woman in the world?

Sky started his show career before he was twelve months old. Mature for his age, he was a real head-turner; tiny ears, square muzzle, shallow mouth, huge hip, and perfect color. Both his parents were champions. Over the next five years, Sky followed in their hoof steps with equal – or greater - success.

Sky was a halter champion, earning a Register of Merit before he was eighteen months old. As a yearling, he was the high point halter stallion of all ages for our multi-state region. Sky was collecting wins; I was learning how to condition and show halter horses. He also started to exhibit a bit more opinion than I was always prepared for. Yet his disposition remained kind. Sky required more direct leadership to get him to go along with my program. Yet he did go along.

Sky was twenty months old when I started him under saddle. It was late December of his yearling year. At the time, I didn't do much preparatory groundwork. I just saddled and moved forward with young horses. After only four times wearing a saddle, four times with a bit in his mouth, and four rides under our belts, Sky could walk on command, jog, side-pass, open and close gates and back. After only four rides! The sixth time I ever saddled him, we delivered Christmas gifts to our neighbors. I wore a backpack loaded with presents and rode Sky. We played Santa together. He was amazing. I had an equine prodigy on my hands.

Less than two weeks into our riding career, Sky and I walked out the front gate of our property onto the gravel road. We hadn't gotten too far when a huge, yellow backhoe rounded a corner and rumbled directly toward us. What in the world would I do? Would Sky spook and run into the street? Buck? With no reasonable option, I sat as calmly as possible and hoped Sky and I would survive this calamity. Had I made a potentially fatal mistake by riding this totally green colt out onto the road?

What happened? Nothing. Sky couldn't care less. His ego wasn't fragile enough to be concerned about some loud, dusty, stinky machine. Sky's legend was already building in my mind. Perhaps that was the day I started going down the wrong path. Or maybe it was a day or two later when Sky and I rode through the high Sonoran Desert north of our property. Our trail passed within six feet of a giant cactus. Just before we got to the twenty-foot-high, multi-armed Saguaro, Sky abruptly stopped. *Why, did he stop?*

Sky was perfectly calm. He looked directly at the cactus, his nose about two feet off the ground in its normal traveling position. Sky didn't move, except to slowly raise his head, examining the cactus from where it started at the ground until his nose pointed skyward, looking to the very top. His curiosity satisfied, Sky assumed his normal traveling position

249

and resumed our walk along the path. If there were any question before, I was now absolutely convinced that Sky was special.

Sky was a specific gift from God; and answer to prayer. If I'd recognized that and accepted it with gratitude and humility, this story would end much differently. But, I didn't.

My failure was one of relationship. I thought I was ready to be his leader. I was not. I determined that Sky would be my horse and forever partner. He could have been. He was prepared to do his part but I was too ignorant and arrogant to do mine. We enjoyed great success, but there was a part of him I never had. Sky would have given it, but I didn't know how to ask for it, to earn it, or deserve it.

I wanted to win. I wanted to make a name for both our horse program and myself. I sacrificed what I'd prayed for - a perfect equine partner. God gave him to me. I wasted the chance. Foolishly, I started Sky's breeding career as a two-year-old, before he fully learned to be a performance horse.

Sky still became a champion. As a weanling. As a yearling. A star pupil when I started him under saddle. A National and World champion reining horse. Sky sired champions. At his first World Show under saddle he tied for Reserve World Champion All-Around Western horse. Sky excelled at everything, but was difficult in some ways. He was always a stallion first and a show horse second. His ground manners were excellent, but periodically he challenged riders, testing their leadership ability.

Little hints that our relationship was not as it should be kept coming but I didn't see them for what they were. Even as a new yearling, Sky wouldn't lunge without a chain - perfect evidence of a hole in the foundation of our relationship. John Lyons personally worked on the lunging issue but couldn't make the connection with Sky. It was the beginning of the break that would keep us from being rightly related and limit the extent to which he and I would go together. Before I could fully repair our foundation, time ran out.

Sky never had a mean hair on him. You could have put a toddler in his stall without concern. Sky would either step around or nuzzle them. He occasionally challenged authority, but if he found the human wanting he simply left the scene. He never tried to bite, kick, or strike. He simply dismissed the person and tried to leave them behind.

My worst mistake was yet to come.

My husband and I moved to Texas in 1999 to concentrate on breeding reining and cutting quarter horses. Sky came along as my horse. We started doing reining maneuvers again and I wanted to be sure he was still good enough for open NRHA (National Reining Horse Association) competition. Upon the advice of a trusted advisor, I took Sky to a trainer I didn't personally know to get checked out. Rather than work through the process with Sky myself, I took the easy way out. After all, I was building a new facility and working on the new program. It was an easy choice for me; disastrous for Sky.

Within a few months, Sky was home again, injured, and forever changed. Sky had never been mean. He still wasn't. Worse, Sky had learned fear. Most horses choose to run when afraid. Sky learned to attack before he was attacked. He was only home a few days when he came at me teeth first when I entered his stall with the cleaning cart. There was fear in his eyes. I'll never know exactly what happened to him, but Sky would never be the same again.

Over time Sky learned to trust me again. His trust didn't extend to my husband or anyone else, and it was no longer a pure trust. Sky was gelded, and we tried to diagnose his physical problem. Great veterinarians tried, but didn't nail down the problem for a long time. I turned him out to

251

pasture for a year. That was hard on a horse raised as a pampered champion with bedded stall and blankets. Sky hated the pasture, but I hoped the time off would repair whatever was wrong.

Eventually we figured it out, did surgery, and Sky was sound again. We were never able to return his complete confidence, and he could be difficult in the barn and under saddle. I loved Sky, but sometimes he was a pain to deal with. My husband and he didn't get along and he wasn't reliable. Wow, that was a hard one to live with. I'd failed him miserably. There was no longer a place in our program for a spotted wonder. He was difficult. I had a full barn. Sky went out to pasture again.

About a year later, I realized that Sky would just get old if he stayed out in the pasture. I brought him back into the barn and started riding him again. My leadership and training skills had improved greatly in the intervening couple of years, and I had new skills to use with Sky. They worked. Sky behaved well, both under saddle and in the barn. He and my husband still weren't friends, but they could coexist. I called Terry Thompson, a trainer who'd known Sky nearly his whole life and who did well with one of Sky's daughters. He tried Sky out for a non-pro client, under the condition that Sky would stay in his barn and under his control as long as he was away from home. I trusted Terry. He lived up to both Sky's expectations and mine. Sky could do almost anything. He was important again. He was a show horse again. All went well for nearly a year.

One day Terry called and said that Sky was nervous at shows and becoming too difficult for a non-pro to handle. I brought him home the next morning. Truthfully, I missed him and was happy he was in my barn again. Still amazingly beautiful, it looked as it Sky and I would finally have our time together.

Sky was back just a few delightful days when I realized he had a problem. I went into his stall to clean as usual. He was perfectly calm, happy to have me there, and promptly ran his head into the handle of the cleaning fork. Sky was blind in one eye. No wonder he was nervous in strange surroundings. He couldn't see anything with his left eye.

A glimmer of returning fear appeared. Sky was sweet except when startled. We worked on trust issues and got along well. I knew our show career was over, but I hoped we could still have the relationship we were meant to have.

The coming downturn in the horse market was getting. As an equine consultant and appraiser, I had a good handle on facts and trends. We started selling our broodmares in 2005, then sold the ranch in 2007. We planned to keep our two best broodmares, but markets kept going down and we eventually sold out completely.

We built a house and small barn on one of our hay fields a mile from the old place. Sky moved with us, taking up residence in one of the four brand new stalls. I was prepared to treat him like the champion he was and continue to work on our relationship. Within a few months, I saw Sky kick out with both hind feet at nothing. He was in his stall and there wasn't even a horse near him at the time. He evidently thought something moved and he had reverted to fight first and ask questions later. Then it happened again. Sky was also losing the sight in his right eye. Fear was causing problems again. This time, I was out of options. Sky wasn't safe in the barn anymore. He could hurt himself and might possibly hurt my husband without meaning to. Sky was put out to pasture once again. His pasture mates were a young donkey and a very passive retired broodmare.

Sky became the boss, leading his contented little herd. Over the next few months, however, the donkey gave Sky increasingly less respect. As his remaining eyesight failed, Sky depended on the old mare to lead him around. Still, he was happy and content for the first time in years. He forgot fear as he became abandoned to dependency. I loved to go to the pasture, hug and pet on him, spending time like we did when he was a new foal. He followed me, just as he had when I taught him to nurse a lifetime ago.

Sky was still gorgeous. He was sweet again. God blessed us both by giving him a handicap that removed his fear and replaced it with sweet trust in me. After examination, I learned he had little, if any, sight remaining. Still, he seemed to get along well in his now-familiar pasture. His guide mare was almost thirty years old, and we knew Sky only had as much time as she did.

Why was I surprised that things didn't work out as planned with Sky? God was at work again. We were leaving for Arizona the next week. It was July; it was hot. I looked out to the pasture a few days before we left and noticed the mare and donkey drinking, but not Sky. He'd been havin difficulty finding the feeder each day. He seemed afraid to put his head into the open trough unless we coaxed him to it. *Perhaps*, I thought, *he's already had a drink and all is well.* The mare walked off. Sky stayed near the waterer but didn't drink. Eventually he moved followed the mare.

Sky's last photo.

The same thing happened later that day. I put a halter on Sky and led him to the waterer to see if he was thirsty. I fully expected him to go with me but not drink. I was wrong again. Sky followed me trustingly, and when I had his nose near the water, he dove in and drank long and deep. Obviously, something had changed. Sky couldn't get water or to his feeder without help. Sky followed me in the open but wouldn't go under the shade.

I was grateful to notice that Sky wasn't drinking before leaving for Arizona. He was spared what might have been a torturous end. This time I didn't fail him. I called the vet. I let Sky go. I was with him at his first breath. I stroked his beautiful head until he drew his last. Finally, I was worthy of the trust he placed in me.

I failed as Sky's leader. I failed to appreciate the answer to my prayer. I was arrogant. God doesn't give open-ended opportunities. When He closes a door it stays closed forever. However, He is faithful to open another and offer another chance to learn the lesson He has for us.

Is it a coincidence that I write this on Good Friday? I don't think so.

I am guilty.

I am ashamed.

I had not done right by Sky. The Lord picked up where I couldn't go to take care of Sky. It was a blessing that such a noble animal wouldn't have to live another decade or more, blind, in the pasture. Sky wasn't born to that life. He was born to relationship with me. I blew it. God was faithful to Sky even when I wasn't. I missed the signs.

God offered me the exact relationship I dreamed of since I was four years old. He gave me just what I asked for. I didn't recognize it. I wasn't ready. Arrogance and pride got in the way.

God, the Father, provided Jesus Christ, His Son, so each of us can enjoy the exact relationship we need. We're all guilty. Only when we feel the burning shame that drives us to our knees can we enter right relationship with Jesus Christ.

Jesus hung on the cross for me. He hung there for you. Don't miss the greatest gift the Father ever gave. Jesus Christ is there for you, but you must renounce your arrogance and pride to receive what you truly desire. Don't make the same mistake I did. Sky wasn't my only failure. There will always be another lesson, another door. But by the grace of God, the sacrifice of His Son, and the tutelage of His Spirit, I have peace, I have joy, and I am saved.

Through the miracle of His grace, I was given another chance. My work of the past thirty-five years came together in the leadership work I do with people and with my amazing grays. Would you be surprised to know no one besides me has ever ridden Bo? That may change someday, but in the meantime, I will not fail him.

I am forever changed by God's amazing grace.

ABOUT THE AUTHOR

Lynn Baber is a best-selling author, World and National Champion horse trainer and breeder, former business consultant, motivational speaker, and serial entrepreneur.

After seven years in ministry, Lynn offers clarity, simplicity, insight, and support to Christians in a post-Christian world.

Lynn also teaches horse owners how to build amazing relationship with their horses by transforming complexity into simple choices.

Lynn and her husband Baber (Larry) share the barn in Weatherford, Texas, with their horses, dogs, and cats.

Connect with Lynn at www.LynnBaber.com

LYNN BABER'S BOOKS

Gospel Horse Series

    Amazing Grays, Amazing Grace – Book 1

    He Came Looking for Me – Book 2

    Discipleship with Horses – Book 3

Christian Living

    Rapture and Revelation

    Fifteen Minutes into Eternity

Ebooks

    The Art of Getting to Yes

    Christian Character

    No Matter What, REJOICE!

95948232R00148

Made in the USA
Columbia, SC
20 May 2018